AS IF THE EARTH MATTERS

Recommitting to Environmental Education

Thom Henley - Kenny Peavy

AS IF THE EARTH MATTERS

Thom Henley - Kenny Peavy

Foundations of the Book

Introduction: Recommitting to Environmental Education

PART I - Awareness

Bonding Activities:

Awareness Activities:

Creating Your Own Curriculum:

Foundations of the Book

Whether you are a veteran of environmental education or new to taking students outdoors, this book will help you organize positive experiences in Nature for your students, friends, children and colleagues. In these pages, you will find ideas designed to arouse your passion for learning and ignite a flame of excitement for teaching.

By using the activities described here, and adapting them to suit your needs and your local environment, you will discover Nature's intricate beauty and subtle mysteries that usually go unnoticed. You will also gain valuable insight into the limitations of classroom instruction and come to realize that a complete and whole education includes getting outside and experiencing the natural world first hand.

The book is divided into three parts: *Awareness, Belonging* and *Stewardship*. The authors believe that inorder to develop a deep connection to the Earth, a person goes through these three sequential stages. He or she must develop a sense of *awareness* of the natural world that surrounds them, be immersed in the outdoors long enough to establish a sense of personal *belonging,* and then finally become *stewards* for the natural world by taking action for conservation and restoration.

Awareness of one's immediate environment can be as simple as noticing the shape of a wispy cloud forming high in the sky or taking time to appreciate the stunning array of colors and patterns exhibited by a neighborhood bird or insect. Most people, focused on the artificial world we have constructed, see only buildings and roads, signs and stores. They are somehow oblivious to the infinite beauty that surrounds them. Becoming aware of who and where you are means looking beyond that backdrop, discovering that there is an enduring world beyond the walls of the buildings we inhabit.

Next, for a person to truly connect and develop a deep appreciation for Nature they must be immersed in the outdoors. There is no substitute for direct experience; immersion is crucial. It is also most often left out in contemporary classroom education.

Immersion simply cannot be done indoors, read in textbooks, viewed in movies or mined from a search engine on the Internet. However, it can take many forms ranging from a leisurely stroll in the local park to a multi-week expedition to a mountain summit, and all forms of being in the environment between those extremes.

Immersion can be recreational, spiritual, social, personal, scientific or simply casual. It is important that it be comfortable and enjoyable in the early stages inorder to promote further exploration. Later, it becomes an opportunity to expand the 'comfort zone' once the individual has developed the self-confidence and skills to push their limits.

As we begin to spend more time outside away from our computers, TVs and video game machines we realize that we too are an integral part of Nature and we come to love this renewed relationship with it. By realizing this we are well on our way to becoming stewards for the Earth and her life giving resources.

Stewardship begins with a realization that the Earth is truly our home and provider of the resources we need to survive and thrive. When a person arrives at this simple and crucial conclusion they become more willing to take action for the preservation and conservation of Nature.

Like immersion, stewardship has a range of possibilities with the crucial factor being that person is willing to invest time and do something. This action can be as simple as planting trees or as involved as restoring a stream habitat with the prospect of returning native fish to a polluted waterway. It might even include volunteering for a conservation organization and devoting your talents and skills toward their mission.

Commitment is the key here and one form stewardship can take is dedicating your time to learn and teach others about Nature through using the activities found within these pages. GET OUTDOORS, have fun, and adapt and use the activities here to enjoy Nature to the fullest!

INTRODUCTION

Renewing the Commitment to Environmental Education

There is really nothing new about the concept of environmental education; it has been integral to the survival of our species, and all species, since the advent of social animals. Grizzly bear cubs, for instance, learn to distinguish more than 300 edible, medicinal and poisonous plants before they leave their mother. Orangutans are known to have the ability to distinguish several hundred edible fruits in the Sumatran and Borneo rainforests in the first three years of their lives. None of this is instinct; it is education in the truest sense of the term.

Indigenous peoples throughout the world are still repositories of a great wealth of natural history knowledge that is vital to their survival. Penan children (the last nomadic forest dwellers of Sarawak, Malaysia) can rattle off the names of more than 200 wild fruits they eat on a regular basis, most of which are unknown to the outside world. Students in modern schools would be hard pressed to do the same, even with access to websites.

The indigenous Moken that live along the Andaman Sea coast of Myanmar and Thailand, can flip through a book illustrating 2,000 marine fish and give a Moken name for every one of them as well as describe where to find each species, how to catch them and what they taste like. No marine biologist in the world, or even the authors of the book, could do the same.

For the first time in human history more people now reside in cities than outside of them. By 2030, it is estimated that 80% of humanity will be urban based. We now feel so comfortably in control of our urban environments with central heating, air conditioning, sanitation facilities, reliable food and water supplies, that we've started to believe that Nature's laws no longer apply to us. People are growing up with little or no opportunities to have direct connections and personal experiences with Nature. More people are disconnected from trees, insects, birds, mountains and rivers than ever before.

from humanity's deliberate attempt to distance itself physically and psychologically from Nature. We have become far too dependent on books, believing absolutely in the power of the printed word even when Nature presents us with lessons to the contrary. Aristotle, for instance, is credited with making the observation that flies have eight legs. For centuries, scholars quoted the great thinker even when students in their classes could swat any annoying fly and count only six legs.

Another challenge we face is that our education systems are increasingly specialized, preparing students for specific roles in complex societies. "My students couldn't tell you a goat from a chicken without reading a DNA sequence," is the way one professor recently summed up this dilemma.

What we teach in classrooms is no longer enough. People need to get outdoors and have a direct experience with Nature and its dazzling diversity of life to ultimately understand their place in the grand scheme of things. The ideas of global warming, greenhouse gases and pollution are abstractions without meaning if students do not have a personal experience and context to relate to.

How can students deeply appreciate the seriousness of pollution if they have never experienced the personal loss of seeing their favorite swimming hole closed due to contaminants? How can someone truly appreciate global biodiversity loss if they have never learned what birds and insects inhabit their own back yards? It really is all connected, but the connections have to be made, witnessed and realized intimately - and absolutely outdoors!

Much of the dilemma modern education faces in teaching environmental education stems

The average student spends less than a few hours a week outside. Even then, that time is mostly spent playing sports on manicured lawns, at artificial playgrounds, riding bicycles or skateboards over city streets, or listening to CD players while walking to and from a closed wall school. Their parents and grandparents may very well be the last generation that spent their hours after school playing in the woods, building huts, catching crayfish and minnows, and running wild until dark.

Children need to get muddy to understand the nature of mud; they need to get uncomfortable at times, to understand what comfort is. We have become a society that increasingly deprives ourselves, and our children, of deprivation.

So what is the solution to this growing dichotomy between humanity and the natural world we are completely part of in spite of our persistent denials? Surely education is crucial in bringing about the consciousness that will be required for our collective survival.

Experiential Education will have to be greatly expanded to bring about the paradigm shift we seek. Recent studies have supported the axiom: "I hear and I forget, I see and I remember, I do and I understand." After one month people remember 14% of what they've heard, 22% of what they saw, 42% of what they saw and heard, 83% of what they heard saw and converted into action, and 91% of what they taught someone else.

A sign above an ancient Korean study center built in the Royal Palace grounds of Seoul in 1777 reads: "Juhamnu" (To Gather the Universe). Can there be a better description of the role of education than this?

It is said that life is not measured by the number of breaths we take, but by the moments that take our breath away. Fully devoted to this sentiment, an elementary school teacher in the Puget Sound region of Washington State gives her students the daily homework assignment of expressing 'Wow!' They are not to bury themselves back in their books after school hours, but to spend enough quality time in Nature that they will experience that involuntary reflex moment and utter the word 'Wow!'

In spite of an optimistic start in the late 1960's and early 1970's, there is a growing feeling today that environmental education has flat lined. Picking up litter and recycling paper and soda pop cans were seen as the early steps necessary to bring about a new environmental ethic in the schools. Unfortunately, more than three decades later, that is still the only environmental focus of most schools.

Students today are being bombarded with so much information on the dismal state of our planet that they are becoming more and more disempowered to do anything about it. Young kids are being confronted with issues of toxins before they've ever beheld a butterfly, or cupped their hands to drink from a clear creek. What seems clearly missing from our intellectual focus on environmental awareness are direct and intimate connections with Nature that result in a heart-felt sense of belonging. Another missing piece of the puzzle, that this book sets out to emphasize, is stewardship activities. Young people need to realize that given half a chance, Nature can be as resilient as youth are, and that with commitment and active involvement, polluted waterways, denuded slopes, and ravaged wildlife populations can often make surprising comebacks.

We hope that the stories, activities and ideas contained in this book will inspire students, parents, teachers and people of all walks of life to take trips outside, have fun and rediscover a deep connection to Nature. More importantly, we hope that teachers everywhere will realize the crucial role they play in changing children's perceptions and will wholeheartedly re-dedicate themselves to environmental education – as if the Earth matters.

PART I
AWARENESS

"In the end we will conserve only what we love,
We will love only what we understand,
We will understand only what we have been taught."

Baba Dioum
African Conservationist (Senegal)

Expanding Awareness

One of the first steps in getting closer to Nature is to become aware. This is often extremely difficult, especially for someone that has spent a majority of their time indoors, eyes locked on a computer game or a TV.

The succession of rapid images flashing in a video game or a music video has conditioned us to expect everything in life to come fast and furious with instant results and super special effects. The challenge is to slow down, calm the mind, and observe our surroundings.

Nature is truly infinite and anyone can discover the beauty contained within a lichen, the dazzling pattern on a dragonfly wing or the spores hidden on the underside of a fern frond.

These activities should engage the senses to their fullest. For them to work best, time should be taken to slow down and escape the hectic pace of life that school and work inevitably demand.

Some of the activities listed in this book as 'energy burners' are simply fun ways for participants to burn off excess energy as a prelude to a quieter, reflective activity.

Becoming aware of what is around us is the first step, and what better way to cultivate awareness than through fun filled exercises!

Bonding

Often the initial step to becoming comfortable with new learning partners and a novel environment is to bond with the people you are exploring Nature with. Leaving out this crucial step may lead to tension or misunderstanding within a group or discomfort in new surroundings. For this reason it is very important to take the time to get to know one another and the space you are learning in and about.

Bonding can be fun and lead to new levels of personal insight and interpersonal understanding.

This section of the book introduces nine effective exercises for outdoor bonding followed by forty-one experiential activities for expanding environmental awareness.

Have fun with them!

15

People to People

A perfect icebreaker, this exercise will get a large group interacting in cooperative, uninhibited, and abjectly silly ways. The instructor starts by getting everyone to clap their hands in unison and repeat everything he or she shouts out. Whenever the leader shouts "People to people," the group must mill about keeping the clapping rhythm going and repeat loudly, "People to people." Once everyone has mastered this simple task, they're asked to pair off while the instructor shows them the chorus section.

"Now hand to hand," the leader shouts while demonstrating a right-to-left and left-to-right hand slap with a partner. The group repeats the phrase and mimics the action. "And toe to toe" (each pair of players touches toes by crossing right over left and left over right). "And friend to friend" (each pair of players shake hands – first right hand, then left hand), "And foe to foe" (each pair does a sparring ritual, touching elbows right over left, then left over right).

Now that the preliminaries are understood, the exercise can begin. As the group mills about keeping time to the instructor's rhyth-

mic clapping and loudly responding to the instructor's chant, "People to people," suddenly a new body part is introduced into the chant: "And knee to knee." Everyone stops beside the person they are closest to at that moment and touches knees while repeating, "And knee to knee," and then immediately repeats the chorus, "And hand to hand, and toe to toe, and friend to friend, and foe to foe."

The instructor's return to the chant, "People to people" signals the renewal of the clapping and the milling about. When the leader returns to shouting, "And knee to knee," everyone stops again with new partners and repeats the knee touch plus one more body part, "And head to head," before repeating the chorus again. Each time the group stops with a new partner the list of body parts grows (i.e., knee, head, shoulder, nose, ear, chin, hip, back, bum). The chorus is always repeated after the litany of body parts and it can be speeded up towards the end. The final chorus is "And hand to hand, and toe to toe, and friend to friend, and foe to foe...And give 'em a hug...And let 'em go!"

Summer/Fall/Winter/ Spring

This is a great activity for groups of twenty or more players in a large open space (beach, meadow, sports field or gymnasium). The instructor asks for a volunteer to come forward to play the role of Princess or Prince Summer/Fall/Winter/Spring.

"Now this is a very 'spinny' character," the instructor begins, "so you must pay careful attention."

The Princess/Prince is asked to extend both arms wide out to the side like the needle of a compass and all players are asked to line up shoulder to shoulder, facing the central character. Everyone with a birthday in June, July, or August lines up in front of the central figure. Those whose birthdays fall in September, October, and November line up in the direction of the Princess's right arm; December, January, February line up behind, and those with birthdays in the spring (March, April, May) line up off the central figure's left arm. The resulting configuration should resemble a large square with all players facing the Princess in the centre. *

"Now organize yourselves chronologically," the instructor continues; "if you're in the winter group be certain the first person in your line-up has the earliest birthday in December and the last person has the latest date in February." All groups do the same. Any two individuals who have the same birth date are asked to raise their arms together to be acknowledged. (Surprisingly, this coincidence is common.)

"Now notice very carefully the player immediately to your right and left - you'll need to find each other again amid considerable confusion," the leader cautions. To give an example, the Princess can be asked to spin on the spot with arms extended while all players scramble to realign themselves to the new position - summer, always in front facing the Princess; fall, always off the right arm; winter, facing the back of the Princess; and spring, off the left arm.

Each of the four groups are then instructed to select a song (or chorus from a song) that symbolizes their season and together as a group rehearse singing loudly. Examples: Summer - "Summertime and the livin' is easy..."; Fall - "Raindrops keep fallin' on my head..."; Winter - "Walkin' in a winter

17

wonderland…"; Spring - "It's May, it's May, the lusty month of May…"

Now that everyone knows their team, their proper line-up and their song, the real action can begin. The Princess spins in a circle with arms extended out to the sides while shouting: "Summer, Fall, Winter, Spring, who will be the first to sing?" Each player must move to their new place (no holding hands here for easier re-alignment) and be standing in their proper place before they start to sing. The instructor or the Princess can point to the winning team after all groups have successfully regrouped. Now the Princess spins off again, this time to another area of the playing field: "Summer, Fall, Winter, Spring, who will be the first to sing?"

This activity can continue until everyone is thoroughly winded - five to six long-distance changes is usually enough. Expect a lot of boisterous singing, hilarity, and general chaos as your group gets to know one another.

Bear, Bug, Frog

This is a large group interactive game like *Eagles and Ravens (pg. 59)* and a good energy burner before *Spirit Spot (pg.133)*. Divide the group into two teams and have them stand facing each other in the middle of a sports field, meadow, or beach. Mark off end zones or "safe" zones at opposite ends of the play area some thirty meters back from the center.

Now demonstrate the three positions that can be taken by the two teams of players:

> **Bear:** players growl while raising both arms overhead, clench teeth and curl fingers like claws of a bear.
> **Bug:** players buzz like biting mosquitoes while extending one index finger in front of the face, like a stinger.
> **Frog:** players quickly crouch on all fours and croak.

Once both teams have practiced all three positions, explain the rules: bears eat frogs; frogs eat bugs; bugs bite bears. Now have each team go into a huddle and choose a sequence of two positions they will assume once they line up at the starting line. For

instance, one team might elect to be bears first, and bugs second. If the other team also chooses bears as their first position, both teams can move on to their second choice. It is extremely rare to have two teams choose the same positions twice, but should this happen they must re-huddle to select their positions again.

As the teams assemble at the starting line the instructor informs them that on the count of three each team will go into their positions – bear, bug, or frog – and respond accordingly: bears chase frogs, frogs chase bugs, bugs chase bears. Any member of a fleeing team caught by the pursuing team before they reach their safe zone becomes a member of the team that caught them. Any member of a team that performs the wrong position (i.e. different from the one the team agreed upon in the huddle) automatically joins the opposing team.

The play gets especially comical when team sizes become very unequal and the team with the smaller size has an instinct to flee even when they are in a position to pursue. Encourage exaggerated body postures and loud vocalizations in the game as it greatly adds to the fun and silliness of the exercise.

Camp Robbers

Anyone who has ever lost precious camp food items to a hungry mouse, bold raven, thieving raccoon or problem bear knows what camp robbers are all about.

In this fast-paced game, all participants get to know the thrill of a successful raid, as well as the fear of getting caught. Divide a large group of ten or more players into two equal teams. Have each team line up and face their opponents from a distance of twelve to sixteen meters. Now go down one line and give each of the players the name of a 'camp robber': blue jay, grey jay, chipmunk, squirrel, mouse, pack rat, raven, fox, raccoon, coyote, wolverine, wolf, bear, weasel, ant, etc. (Try to use the names of animals from your bio-region.) Now give the same names in the same order to the members of the opposing team – starting at the opposite end of their line up.

The instructor has a bag of treats (peanuts in the shell, oranges, bananas, or wrapped candies) which are set on the ground, one at a time, between the two teams. The object of the game is to be the most successful camp robber. When the instructor shouts a name at random, e.g., "Pack rat!" both pack rat players must race to steal the food.

This is a game of stealth as much as of speed because the food can be stolen back from the first person who snatched it simply by tagging that person before they return to their place in the line-up. One must not touch the opponent, however, until the opponent has snatched the food item. To do so results in the opponent taking the food uncontested.

This is the perfect game to burn off a lot of frenzied energy before meal time and, as one might imagine, hunger is the best motivator for a good 'camp robber.'

Don't Bungle the Jungle

While this activity primarily focuses on group interactive fun, it does further environmental awareness. Any number of habitats can be chosen as the theme (e.g., *Don't Bungle the Bog, Don't Bungle the Beach, Don't Bungle the Boreal Forest),* and the exercise can be worked in as a play break from more formal studies.

Start with all players forming a large circle, with the instructor standing alone in the center. The leader closes his or her eyes and spins in a circle with one arm pointing outward. The person in the circle of players who is being pointed to when the leader stops will become the centerpiece for a group activity by the two people immediately beside them. For instance, if the leader shouts "Gibbons," as he or she stops with the pointing arm, the person pointed to would immediately have to raise arms over head, and make gibbon calls while those on the each side would rush in to stroke the under side and arms of the central actor (like group grooming for lice). The last person of the three involved to get into proper position will have "bungled the jungle" and must replace the person at center circle. Each time the center player closes their eyes, spins around and points, they must shout out a new species to be pantomimed by the person being pointed to and the people to their immediate left and right.

Eight to twelve characters can be demonstrated by the instructor at the start of the session, and the group can always be encouraged to come up with characters of their own. The following examples relate to the jungles of Borneo:

Elephant: Central person extends locked arms to form the trunk while players on either side extend both arms to form huge elephant ears. (Example:above)

Sago Palm: All three players face same direction and sway their bodies in unison like palm trees in the wind.

Hornbill: Central person uses hands to form a beak in front of face while those beside raise and lower outreached arms like a bird in flight.

Gibbon: Central person holds one or both arms in the air (like hanging from a limb) while side players groom them.

Termites: All three people bend over in same direction and form a line of moving termites.

Crocodile: Central person extends both arms to become jaws while side players use cupped hands to simulate bulging eyes.

Dung Beetle: All three players line up behind one another, one on knees, one crouched, one standing erect. Each projects bent arms forward and moves them in unison, like the six legs of the beetle. (Example:right)

Penan: (These Borneo forest dwellers are superb marksmen with blowpipes and very affectionate with one another). All three players simulate shooting a blowpipe, then hug one another.

Strangler Fig: Central person raises arms high overhead to become the host tree while side players entwine arms and legs as the strangling fig.

If all three players react in unison to form their configuration correctly, then the person in the middle of the circle of players keeps repeating their turn, pointing and naming a position until someone finally 'bungles.'

An index card listing of all the possible configurations is sometimes helpful to remind the central person of all the possibilities.

Hungry Hawk, Mother Mouse

Hungry Hawk, Mother Mouse is another fast-paced activity, popular with pre-teen groups. A beach, meadow, or large sports field is required for this exercise.

Choose two participants (male and female) to be hungry 'hawks', while a third person (with strong maternal instincts) becomes a protective 'mother mouse'. All other participants become 'baby mice' lining up behind their 'mother', holding the waist of the person in front of them.

The object of the game is for the 'hawk' to grab the last 'mouse' in the line-up and take it off to its nest (a pre-determined spot in the area of play). If you have participants who have difficulty running, they can play the role of 'baby hawks' in the nest. They simulate eating each 'mouse' by tickling the player brought to the 'nest'. The hungry 'hawks' take turns leaving the nest to chase after mice. They repeat this pursuit until all the 'baby mice', and finally the 'mother', are captured.

The 'mother mouse' is very protective, constantly trying to defend her young by getting in the way of the 'hawk' player. While trying to block the 'hawk's' attack, the 'mother mouse' must be careful not to break up her family of 'mice'. To better secure the handhold of the first 'mouse' behind her, the 'mother mouse' grips those hands firmly against her waist with her own hands. So she can never use her hands to struggle with the 'hawk' player.

While this game may seem to put the 'hawks' in a position of unfair advantage, it really comes down to a question of stamina. Very often the 'hawks' will tire before all the 'mice' have been captured. Try this game several times with different 'hawk' players, or until everyone is thoroughly tuckered out.

Cat & Mouse

This is another large group exercise that helps create a team dynamic while engaging in silly fun. You will need approximately 18-22 participants for this activity for it to be really effective.

With a group of 18 players, for instance, have two fast runners stand off to one side while the remaining 16 line up military style, one behind the other, in rows of four. Just like in the Army, they must be arms length apart from one another in both directions. To test this, have them all face you with arms outstretched and finger tips touching; then on your drill sergeant-like command have them: "Face right". Once again every participant's finger tips should be touching with new partners. Try it again in reverse: "Face left!" They should now be back in their original position.

Now that your maze is properly set up, choose your two remaining participants to become the 'cat' and the 'mouse'. Different colored headbands can be used to distinguish them. The object of the game is for the mouse player to run through the maze in a clever enough way to avoid being caught by the 'cat'. Neither the 'cat' nor the 'mouse' can break through the maze where two students's finger tips are touching. They can only run through the open passage ways and around the ends of each row of players.

The mouse player, of course, has a secret escape route - as all mice do. This player can change the direction of the maze any time they wish by simply shrieking, "Eek, eek!" anytime the 'cat' is in too hot a pursuit. Foiled again, the cat player has to start over with a new strategy. The action gets very cartoon-like, much to the delight of the whole group.

Sometimes a good 'mouse' is just too clever to ever get caught by the 'cat'. At times like this the instructor can step into the position of one of the players forming the maze, and free that person to become a second 'cat'. The 'mouse' is now about to meet its match.

Some of the participants that make up the maze will want a turn playing the 'cat' or the 'mouse', but the activity doesn't usually carry on too long once the maze participants get weary from holding their arms stretched outright.

Ant & Elephant

"Let's play more games," participants at Ghost River Rediscovery in Alberta, Canada demanded of their group leader near the close of a full day of enjoyed group exercises. "You guys come up with a game," the facilitator responded. "But we can't think of any new games," came the response from the kids. "Think of an animal then," they were told.

A young boy looked down at his feet and answered, "An ant!" "Make up a game with an ant then," the instructor encouraged them. "But there aren't any games with ants," they protested. "Think of another animal then," the facilitator prodded. "An elephant," one of the participants said to be as ridiculous as they possibly could. "Good," the facilitator responded, "use your imagination and make up a game with an ant and an elephant." The result - *Ant & Elephant* - has become an all-time favorite activity at Rediscovery camps world wide.

You will need a minimum of 10-12 participants for this exercise. Divide the group into two 'ant colonies'. They can even be given colored head bands to distinguish them as red and black ants. Now set out two circular areas, approximately 20-30 meters apart, on opposite ends of a nice grassy playing field. Rope, survey tape or even blindfolds tied together can be used to simulate each 'ant colony hole'. The 'hole' needs to be wide enough to set a large person lying down inside it.

Now choose two large people of equal size from each 'colony' and set them out in the center of the play area, lying comfortably on their backs and about one meter apart from each other. The object of the game is for each 'ant colony' to crawl on all fours and, without using their hands, devise some way to lift their 'elephant' and transport it as food back to their hole. The result, as you might well imagine, is hilarious.

Prior to starting the activity it is important to give each 'ant colony' time to bond and devise their strategy. Just as real life ants use their antennae to ensure every individual ant they encounter is a member of their colony, so too do the participants need to develop a strong colony sense before they set out to get their 'elephant.' Rolling an 'elephant' back to an 'ant hole' is an obvious option, but the 'ants' will soon discover it's not as fast as finding a way to lift their 'elephant' onto their backs to transport it back to the hole. The 'elephants' are deliberately placed close to one another to make the task of the 'ants' more difficult.

Ant & Elephant combines all the characteristics of a good bonding exercise; it involves group planning, cooperation, physical contact and a childlike sense of fun.

Save the Earth

We're not talking about planetary survival here. The Earth doesn't need to be "saved", nor are humans capable of saving it. What we do need to save is the Earth as we like it to be - with its climate, air, water, soil and biodiversity intact - and as we've always known it. If we mess that up, the planet will shake us off as quickly as it has discarded countless species before us.

It is sobering to realize that all species ultimately go extinct, just as it is encouraging to know that most species survive an average 3-5 million years before their demise. Hominoids (upright apes) have only been populating the Earth for approximately 2 million years, and Homo sapiens ('wise' man) have only been around a mere 100,000 years. It's entirely possible that the best years for our species still lie ahead. How wisely we address the dilemmas facing humanity in this century will ultimately decide how worthy we are of survival.

Save the Earth is a sport-like activity that should leave a lasting impression on all its players. You will need a large field and a ball for this game, basketball-size or bigger. A strong, inflatable Earth globe is ideal, but any large blue rubber ball can be painted (green and brown for land masses, and white for swirling clouds) to resemble the Earth as viewed from space.

Before the start of the exercise, challenge your students to identify the gravest dangers humanity faces today. War, famine, overpopulation, deadly disease, genocide, biodiversity loss, climate change, ozone depletion and growing inequality between the haves and have-nots, are likely to top most lists.

Print out names of these 'Earth Dangers' on large index cards or construction paper and attach them with safety pins to the shirt front of half the players. The other half of the students will become the 'Earth Savers'. They can be distinguished by use of blue or green cloth strips worn as head bands or arm bands.

The game is played like football or rugby with two end zones. The object of the game is for the 'Earth Savers' to move their Earth ball from one end of the field to the other. The 'Earth Dangers' have the objective of impeding the path of their opponents, either by tagging them, or stealing the ball. The rules of engagement are as follows:

- an 'Earth Saver' can hold or run with the ball up to 3 seconds before they must pass it to another on their team

- an 'Earth Saver' tagged by an 'Earth Danger' must forfeit the ball to his/her opponent and return to their end zone to start over

- an 'Earth Danger' player that tags out an 'Earth Saver' can kick the ball on the ground back in the direction the 'Earth Savers' are advancing from. Only another 'Earth Saver' can retrieve this ball.

- if a passed ball is intercepted by an 'Earth Danger', that person runs with it back to the 'Earth Saver' end zone for the play to start over.

Needless to say, it is nearly impossible for the 'Earth Savers' to cross the field to the opposite end zone under these stacked rules. Allow for time outs every 6-10 minutes so the players can catch their breath and have 60 seconds to discuss strategies in a huddle. Hopefully, at some point the 'Earth Savers' will come to the realization that their

most determined efforts are doomed to fail unless they modify their attack.

The rules state that a single player holding the ball may do so for only 3 seconds before they must pass it to another. But what if the entire team decides to move the ball as a tight group? No individual player could be tagged out as other players' hands could support the ball the moment any one player is about to be tagged. As long as the ball keeps moving from hand to hand within the central group of players, the 'Earth Savers' would be able to cross the field.

Another possible strategy would be to position two players in the center of a circle of 'Earth Savers' all holding hands. The center players could hand the ball back and forth to each other every three seconds while the circle fights off 'Earth Dangers' as their team crosses the field. There are other possible strategies that the 'Earth Savers' could devise to be successful.

The objective of this activity is not a sporting event at all, but for the players to realize the extraordinary level of creativity and cooperation that will be required for humanity to save itself from the dangers it faces.

Following the game, gather everyone together to de-brief and process what happened.

Was there a sudden change in consciousness of one or more individuals that brought about a successful strategy? Are there any parallels in human society that give us cause to hope that a dire situation might suddenly be turned around? Are such changes more likely to be brought about from individual or group initiatives?

Be sure to address each of the 'Earth Dangers' the students wrote on their cards. Which of these issues do they feel is being adequately addressed? Which are not? What are the impediments to this? What can they, as students, do to help?

29

Alien Ecosystem

Age Level: elementary / middle (6-13 years)
Skills/Subject Areas: science, self expression, tuning in to Nature, relationships in Nature observation, cooperative learning, peer teaching
Eco-Concepts:
   Diversity - differences in living things allow for the success of all life
   Interdependence - all things are connected to and depend on other living things
   Community - animals and plants live together in special areas that meet their needs
Required Materials: 1 meter loop of survey tape per student, 1 hand lens per student, 7-12 toothpick flags per student
Prep Time: low – less than 10 minutes

Description:

Alien Ecosystem is ideal for a close examination of a sphagnum bog, alpine meadow, tundra, or a rock face adorned with mosses and lichens.

"Ahhh, here we are deep in the heart of the bog; what a weird-looking place", the instructor announces as participants are led to the site for the activity. "Doesn't it seem like we're on some kind of lost planet? Look at the strange shapes of those dwarf trees and this unearthly red and orange moss. Oh oh, look out! Watch where you step," the instructor warns, "there are animal-eating plants living here."

Give out space explorer kits to all participants and ask them to spread out in search of an alien ecosystem. The kits should contain a jeweler's lens for close observation and a one-meter length of survey tape tied together to delineate the boundaries of the study plot.

"The first wonder on my planet is the dark hole of the mighty centipede: there are the pine-needle steps for its hundred legs," says a participant as he points to a toothpick flag he's placed within his survey tape circle. "Wow, that's so cool!" says another kid taking the 'trip' to his buddies 'planet'. The Alien Ecosystem explorer points to the next toothpick flag.

"You'll need the lens to see the second wonder. See the drops hanging on the moss. They're like giant diamonds on this planet."

Staff members should also take tours of each of the youngsters' alien ecosystem and ask questions to get them thinking: "Why do you suppose the plants on this planet have hairy leaves and stems? Do you think this planet is very dry? Windy? What is its atmosphere like? How cold do you think it gets here? How do the plants on your planet reproduce? What eats them?" The questions can lead into complexities such as the high acidity of a bog, the short growing season of the alpine and tundra, wind desiccation, and the role of lichens in breaking down rocks and absorbing nitrogen directly from the air.

Don't dwell on the lessons. The main purpose of *Alien Ecosystem* is to open one's eyes to the natural world - especially the micro-world we rarely take notice of. Young children generally use far more imagination on this exercise than do teens or adults.

Bamboo Cycle

Age Level: elementary / middle (6-13 years)
Skills/Subject Areas: science, P.E., energy burner, knowledge of flora and fauna, relationships in Nature
Eco-Concepts:
   Cycles - Nature works in cycles; the building materials for life must be used over and over again
   Interdependence - all things are connected to and depend on other living things
   Community - animals and plants live together in special areas that meet their needs
Required Materials: activity cards (photocopy, enlarge and laminate pgs.33-34)
Prep Time: medium (15-20 min.)
Classroom Adaptations/Variations: challenge students to learn more about each species that uses bamboo or investigate human uses of bamboo

Description:

There are many kinds of cycles in Nature. The water cycle and nitrogen cycle spring easily to mind, but there are also others. Plants, for instance, display seasonal cycles, often going dormant in winter months in temperate latitudes only to spring back to life when the weather warms. Tropical plants can display even more fascinating cycles.

Consider bamboo, one of the fastest growing and most useful plants in the world. (Burmese bamboo can grow up to 1 meter per day!) Bamboo species vary considerably in their life expectancies, but 12-15 years is a good average. People who use bamboo as part of their home landscaping are always dismayed to see a healthy stand of this elegant plant – that has thrived for a decade or more – suddenly produce seed and die.

When bamboo produces seed in its native Southeast Asian forest habitat, it provides a rich food source for large troops of Pig-tail macaque monkeys that climb the sturdy stalks to reach the hanging clusters of grass-like seeds. As the seeds fully ripen and fall to the ground, they become like chicken-scratch for increasingly large flocks of Red jungle fowl - the ancestor to all domestic chickens. Jungle fowl can produce broods of 15-20 chicks several times a year, so in bamboo die-back years their populations explode with the sudden abundance of feed.

When bamboo seeds sprout they are the favored food of Mouse deer, one of the world's smallest hoofed animals. Barking deer, a somewhat larger species, graze on young bamboo shoots as they grow their first meter. Sambar deer, the largest of Southeast Asia's deer species, graze on bamboo up to two meters tall.

But even as bamboo grows out of browsing reach of the tallest deer, it is still not safe from foraging. Asian elephants love bamboo and eat it by the tons. They often bulldoze stands 3-8 meters tall with their massive bulk and weight, just to get at the plant's tender tips. Langurs, or leaf monkeys, also relish bamboo leaves. They can often be seen perched high atop the swaying stalks of mature stands foraging for hours on the rich foliage.

Throughout most of its life, bamboo reproduces by means of underground shoots called rhizomes. These tubers, rich in carbohydrates, are the main-stay of the burrowing Bamboo rat, yet another species dependent on this remarkable plant. When a grove of bamboo has grown very large and is fully mature in 12-15 years, it will stop reproducing by rhizomes and suddenly go to seed, renewing the cycle in turn for all the species it has benefited.

Bamboo Cycle is a large group activity that helps youngsters not only understand the stages of bamboo growth and reproduction, but the many species of animals that benefit from each stage of the plant's life cycle.

Bamboo Cycle is an activity that can be played in groups of 8, 16, 24, or 32 players. All players sit in a circle while one additional player stands in the center of the circle, symbolically representing the bamboo grove. This center player holds large picture cards each representing one of the eight stages in bamboo development: 1) sprouting seeds, 2) one meter growth, 3) two meter growth, 4) 3-8 meter growth, 5) mature stand, 6) rhizome production, 7) producing seeds, and 8) shedding seeds.

Mouse Deer

Barking Deer

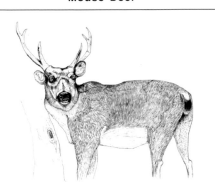

Sambar Deer

Asian Elephant

Langur

Bamboo Rat

Pig-tail Macque

Jungle Fowl

Sprouting Seeds

1 Meter Growth

2 Meter Growth

3 - 8 Meter Growth

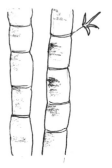

Mature Stand

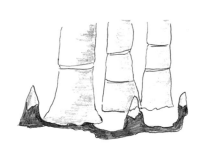

Rhizome Production

Producing Seed

Shedding Seeds

The center circle player is assigned the task of shuffling the cards (face down) and arbitrarily selecting one to hold up for all to see during each round of the activity. All other players sit in a large circle around this central player. To begin a teacher or facilitator counts off each player in the circle 1-8, assigning each student a card with the name and picture of an animal that depends on bamboo: 1) Mouse deer, 2) Barking deer, 3) Sambar deer, 4) Asian elephant, 5) Leaf monkey, 6) Bamboo rat, 7) Pig-tail macaque, and 8) Red jungle fowl.

It is best to keep the order the same as you proceed from one team of eight players sitting in the circle to the next. You need at least two teams of 8 players to make the game challenging, but it can be played with 3 or more teams of eight.

Once everyone has their cards and knows the rules, the bamboo grove player in the center shuffles and draws a card. Holding it high and turning for all to see, he or she announces the stage of the bamboo growth. If, for instance, the card reads "shedding seeds", every player in the circle holding a card that designates them to be a 'Red jungle fowl' must jump up and run completely around the outer circle of players. Once they return to the spot where they were seated, they can then enter the circle and run to the center player. The first 'Red jungle fowl' to reach the 'bamboo grove' scores a point for their team. If three or more teams are playing, then the first player to reach the center can score 3 points, the second player scores 2 points, and the third player sores 1 point. The total score at the end of 10-15 rounds of play will determine the winning team.

The object of the game, of course, is not about points or winning, but learning the dynamics between animal populations and changing habitat. When everyone is good and winded from the physical part of the exercise, have a discussion on plant cycles and animal relationships more pertinent to your bioregion.

While temperate latitude examples are usually less complex than tropical ones, they are nonetheless interesting. Deer, for instance, browse oak tree saplings, caterpil-

lars forage on growing oak leaves, woodpeckers seek out grubs under mature bark, and squirrels depend heavily on the tree's acorns during the fruiting cycle.

Challenge the students to come up with examples of their own.

Beach-Life Bingo

Age Level: any age (6 and up)
Skills/Subject Areas: science
Eco-Concepts
　　Diversity - differences in living things
　　allow for the success of all life
　　Community - animals and plants live
　　together in special areas that meet their
　　needs
Required Materials: hand made bingo
cards and game pieces (shells, pine
cones, etc.)
Prep Time: high - 30 minutes or more
Classroom Adaptations/Variations: students can make their own bingo cards by
studying a specific ecosystem (i.e. desert,
inter-tidal, rainforest etc.) and illustrating the
flora and fauna of that ecosystem

Description:

Beach-Life Bingo reinforces lessons in marine biology and food gathering. It also
serves as a great indoor activity on a stormy
day. The bingo cards are larger than normal
and have colored pictures of marine life in
each of the squares usually reserved for
numbers. The names and pictures of all
these marine creatures are printed on cards
and drawn randomly from a barrel, just as in
regular bingo. Of course, no two playing
cards are identical, so the same elements of
chance and luck prevail.

If the caller should pull the card for Pisaster
starfish, the players now have to distinguish
between several other species of starfish:
bat stars, sunflower stars, and blood stars.
If the group has too much trouble with this,
the caller can show the picture on the name
card.

Clam shells are used in place of bingo chips.
To expand the learning potential of the game,
the participants set clam shells face down
on those marine creatures living primarily on
sand or sand/mud beaches, and face up if
they are found on solid-rock habitat.

Of course, this concept can be applied
equally well to any ecosystem with its community of plants and animals. Use pine-cone
bingo chips in *Forest-Life Bingo* or stones
for *Desert-Life Bingo*.

Standard variations on the game can be used
to determine winners: one line in any direction, a cross, vertical, horizontal, or blackout
bingo, where all squares must be covered.
Prizes can range from sweets to a certificate good for a free turn off dishwashing
duty in a camp setting.

Bear Nose

Age Level: any age (6 and up)
Skills/Subject Areas: science
Eco-Concept:
 Adaptation - everything has evolved
 to fit how and where it lives
Required Materials: forest fragrances collected on site
Prep Time: low - less than 10 minutes
Classroom Adaptations/Variations:
class discussion, research animal species that depend primarily on smell, or the anatomy and physiology of.the olfactory system

Description:

We've all heard the childhood song: "The bear went over the mountain... to see what he could see - and all that he could see... was the other side of the mountain." A much better portrayal of bear behavior would be the lyrics: "The bear went over the mountain... to see what he could smell from 50 km away." Of course, that doesn't rhyme, so it's unlikely to catch on.

Bears do have amazing olfactory facilities that help offset their notoriously poor eyesight. Trappers and miners in the Yukon and Alaska talk of drawing in bears from a 100 km radius simply by frying bacon for breakfast in their bush camps.

To help youngsters realize how important our own sense of smell is in determining subtle differences in Nature, take them to a forest setting and have them take turns sniffing natural aromas. *Forest Fragrances (pg. 66)* is a good lead-in to this exercise as it gets the olfactory glands more attuned to subtle differences in smell than they normally are.

Tell your students that they are now to imagine themselves as bears, with a sense of smell many times better than humans. Have a second student gently use their hands to cover a participant's eyes while the instructor offers that person a distinct scent to

breathe in. (Be careful in presenting the forest scents so no part of the object comes in contact with the face, or they will have the advantage of a touch clue.) Items from the forest that work well for this exercise are: fungus, rotting wood, mud, flowers (not endangered), tree pitch, berries, pine, spruce, cedar, or other leaves that are crushed to bring out their full fragrance.

Once each student confirms that they have their scent registered in their mind, their eyes are uncovered and they must go out into the surrounding forest to find a sample of the same object.

It is common for students to think that all evergreens have the same smell, and they

often return with a species different from the sample they were given to sniff. Send them out again until they get it right. Others may need to return to refresh their memory by sniffing their object a second or third time. To better facilitate this, the instructor should keep all of the scent objects in small plastic bags, so the smells do not transfer from one object to another and they are easy to retrieve for those needing another sniff.

Bigfoot

Age Level: any age (6 and up)
Skills/Subject Areas: science, observation skills, knowledge of local flora and fauna, tuning in to Nature
Eco-Concepts:

> **Cycles** - Nature works in cycles; the building materials for life must be used over and over again
> **Diversity** - differences in living things allow for the success of all life
> **Change** - everything is in the process of becoming something else

Required Materials: survey tape, notepad, pen, hand lens per participant
Prep Time: medium - 15-20 minutes
Classroom Adaptations/Variations: sketch or take digital photographs of the flora and fauna while in the field then use field guides to identify your sketches when you return to the classroom

Description:

Everyone has heard the tales of Sasquatch or 'Bigfoot', the large ape-like creature believed by some to inhabit North America's Pacific Northwest. Let all the participants imagine themselves to be a Sasquatch. Give

them each a notepad and pen, a magnifying glass, a loop of survey tape (or even a coat hanger bent into the shape of a Sasquatch footprint). Then invite them to spread out in any direction they choose, taking giant 'Bigfoot' steps as they go. Before everyone gets too far apart, the instructor shouts, "Stop, Bigfoot!"

Now all the players are instructed to squat down beside the spot where their next footprint would have been and mark it by carefully setting down their 'Bigfoot' step. Then they take out pen, paper and magnifying glass to record as many different things as they can find: cones, needles, seeds, twigs, flowers, leaves, spiders, ants, mushrooms, lichens, liverwort and more inside their designated study plot.

If the participants don't know the names for all the items they should try to describe them as best they can. The instructor should also rotate from site to site, pointing out details and interesting features of the forest floor the students wouldn't otherwise be aware of. Examples: "Look here, you have a centipede crawling into your 'Bigfoot' step. Notice the black and yellow coloration. That's a warning signal to birds. 'Don't eat me, I taste awful!' Pick up the centipede and smell it to get some idea of how it might taste. And look, over here, near your 'Bigfoot' toe you have a lichen, one of the oldest plants on the planet. It is actually two plants appearing as one - a partnership between algae and fungus. A relationship that's good for both parties is called symbiosis."

Groups may spend thirty to fifty minutes engrossed in a world they normally walk over quickly. A list of forty items or more is not uncommon in an old-growth forest; much less is found in second-growth sites.

Once the whole surface of a 'Bigfoot' step has been surveyed, invite the participants to look a few centimeters underground for a whole list of objects: soil, roots, mould, centipedes, worms, mites, ants and spider eggs, etc. Encourage everyone to put their noses down near the ground and have a deep smell of good, clean earth. "Just think," the instructor concludes, "most of the creatures that live in the temperate forests live underground – but our magnifying lenses aren't powerful enough to see them."

Because Sasquatches don't like their whereabouts known, it is important to conceal all signs of one's 'Bigfoot' step before leaving the site.

Bug Bites

Age Level: any age
Skills/Subject Areas: science, observation
Eco-Concepts:
   Diversity - differences in living things allow for the success of all life
   Interdependence - all things are connected to and depend on other living things
   Community - all living things interact with other living things in areas that meet their special needs
   Adaptation - everything is designed to fit how and where it lives
Required Materials: print out of insect feeding guilds (found below)
Time Commitment: low
Classroom Adaptations/Variations: while in the classroom design an imaginary pattern of insect feeding and see if you can find it outside.

Description:

Do all people eat the same?
No, some people use chopsticks others use a fork and spoon while still others use their hands. Insects are like that too. Many different types of insects eat differently. Some insects stick a long mouth (shaped like a needle) into a leaf and suck out the juice, much like humans drink through a straw. Some insects chew their way in between the layers of a leaf like digging a tunnel while others eat big holes all the way from top to bottom. We can tell this by noticing the marks they leave on the leaves they eat.

Look around and see if you can notice these different types of insect feeding:

A leaf miner

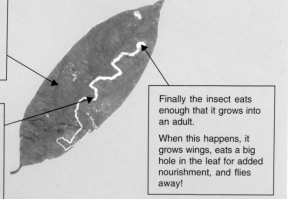

Leaf miners are called that because they appear to 'mine' a tunnel through a leaf.
They do this by eating their way through the layers of the leaf and leaving a trail behind them!

It's kind of like how humans mine through the earth and make a tunnel

Notice how the 'tunnel' that the insect has created is getting bigger.

Why do you think this happens?

(Because it's growing while it eats and needs a bigger tunnel!)

Finally the insect eats enough that it grows into an adult.

When this happens, it grows wings, eats a big hole in the leaf for added nourishment, and flies away!

Pit Feeder

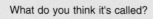

You'll probably see a lot of this type of feeding in the forest. It's very common.

What do you think it's called?

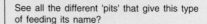

See all the different 'pits' that give this type of feeding its name?

Insects that eat this way essentially eat small little holes throughout the leaf.

That's why they're called pit feeders.

A Skeletonizer

Why do you think this type of insect feeding is called a skeletonizer?

When you see this type of insect feeding in the forest you'll notice that all that's left of the leaf are its ribs and veins!

Insects that eat like this are called 'skeletonizers' because they eat all the nutritious good green leaf and leave the bare leaf skeleton behind.

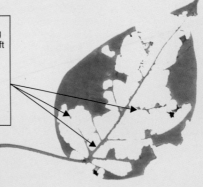

Camera Kids

Age Level: any age (6 and up)
Skills/Subject Areas: knowledge of local flora and fauna, tuning in to Nature, observation skills, bonding
Eco-Concept:
    Diversity - differences in living things allow for the success of all life
Required Materials: none
Prep Time: none
Classroom Adaptations/Variations: after the activity students can take actual digital photos of what they observed and research the names, ecological relationships and importance of the flora/fauna they examined

Description:

As any Nature photographer can attest, cameras can be an effective tool for putting people in more intimate contact with the natural world. Close-up lenses help us peer closely into Nature's intricacies and beauty. *Camera Kids* literally opens eyes to Nature, with no camera at all.

Have everyone find a partner and decide who in each pair will be the 'photographer' and who will be the 'camera'. Demonstrate how a human camera works by gently holding the sides of the head of a partner from behind.

"Now, as in all good cameras, the shutter stays closed [close your partner's eyes]. To open the shutter and take a picture, you simply push one of your partner's ear lobes while saying 'click' and close it by releasing the earlobe with another 'click.' This motion opens and closes the eyes for the desired exposure length - usually one or two seconds. At all other times the 'camera's' eyes are closed."

Once everyone has mastered the technique, ask the 'photographers' to go off with their 'cameras' and photograph the three most beautiful images they can find. Flowers, ferns, moss and tree bark all make for wonderful close-ups; position the 'camera' partner's head directly over the object before releasing the earlobe shutter. Panning shots of landscapes, treetops, creeks and ocean vistas can also be shot video style, with a three- to four-second time exposure. A creative photographer might wish to photograph the leaves floating on a rain puddle with the reflection of the camera and photographer looking back at the lens from the water. As in real photography, creativity, composition and lighting are the keys to good images.

Once the 'photographers' have completed the three assigned photos, they become the 'cameras', and their partners lead them off on a photo session.

As soon as each team returns after completing their assignment, hand out blank index cards and colored pencils or pens, so that each 'camera' can process the one image in their mind they liked best. 'Photographers' should not view the pictures as their 'cameras' are 'processing'.

When everyone has finished their drawings, gather the entire group in a circle and begin passing all the images clockwise for everyone to have a look. On the second rotation of the images, ask the 'photographers' to pull out the image that they took (the one their 'camera' processed). It is interesting to see if a 'photographer' can recognize their own work as interpreted by another.

As a nice closing to this exercise, have the 'cameras' autograph their 'photos' and dedicate it to their 'photographers', "With love, your camera," before presenting them as a memento.

Canopy Levels

Age Level: elementary / middle (6-13 years)
Skills/Subject Areas: science, cooperative learning
Eco-Concepts:
   Diversity - differences in living things allow for the success of all life
   Community - animals and plants live together in special areas that meet their needs
Required Materials: rainforest diorama, species cards, canopy level cards
Prep Time: high - 30 minutes or more

Description:

Anyone that ever has an opportunity to stand on a vantage point looking out over a broad expanse of tropical rainforest, can't help but notice that there appears to be different layers in the canopy - some trees clearly tower above others. Although tropical ecosystems are so immensely complex they defy simple description, there is a tendency for humans to want to put some semblance of order to things. Describing the sophisticated tapestry of tropical rainforests in various levels is one such attempt.

Biologists generally recognize five levels of a rainforest: 1) emergent trees which rise above the canopy, 2) the upper canopy that forms a continuous cover, 3) the lower canopy made up of shade-tolerant species and young emergent trees, 4) an understory of shrubs, and 5) the forest floor.

Canopy Levels is an activity designed to help students, even in a school setting, to gain a much greater appreciation for the wonderful diversity of living things found at each of these levels. The students themselves can help create a painting of a forest diorama on large roll paper that can later be taped to a high wall for this exercise. It is better yet to design a profile of a tropical rainforest on a large cotton sheet, or canvas mural so that it can be easily folded up, stored and used time and time again.

The rainforest canopy mural should not contain images of animals found in the forest as these will be added during the exercise itself. You will need to find images of at least 6-8 species of animals found at each of the five levels of the forest. Color photographs, mounted on construction board and laminated for long term wear, are ideal. Each species card should have the name of the species printed on the back, along with a bit of information about the role that species plays in the forest ecosystem. Each card also needs to have a strip of Velcro attached to it, and a corresponding strip of Velcro sewn or glued to the location on the mural where that species would normally be found.

Examples for species found at each level of a Southeast Asian rain forest might be:

Emergent Trees:
gibbons, eagles, hornbills, bees, leaf cutter insects and sunbirds

Upper Canopy: flower peckers, barbets, fruit doves, fruit bats, large squirrels, langurs and flying lemurs

Lower Canopy: butterflies, tree frogs, gliding lizards, woodpeckers, trogons, flycatchers, bulbuls, clouded leopard, slow loris, civets, tree shrews and smaller squirrels

Understory: elephants, rhino, sambar deer, barking deer, mouse deer, sun bear, tiger, porcupine and marten

Forest Floor: beetles, scorpions, ants, millipedes, leeches, tarantulas and scaley anteater

The bleachers of a school gymnasium work very well for this activity as it is possible to position students at five levels to correspond with the five levels on the mural mounted in front of them. Use signs to mark out each canopy level on the steps or bleachers where you conduct the exercise. It would be even better to conduct this exercise outdoors on a hillside where students could be placed according to their canopy level and the mural could be hung from a rope between two trees.

The activity is played by designating equal numbers of students to sit in five different rows to correspond with the five canopy levels. Each student is presented with an animal card that corresponds with their level.

They are to read the information on the back of their species card, but they are not to let others see it.

The game starts by asking volunteers to come forward in front of the mural to pantomime their animal. All students that are seated start to guess what that animal might be. The first person that guesses correctly scores a point for their team, and the privilege of being the next to mime their animal.

Once a student has had their animal correctly identified, they then attach it to the mural at the correct canopy level with the aid of the Velcro on the back of their card, or by sewing the piece onto the mural. Sometimes a small ladder is required to help students place their animal cards at the highest canopy levels.

It is best not to show the total scores being tallied for each canopy level team until the close of the exercise. It's also necessary at times to exclude from guessing the students that are part of the level the person doing the pantomime comes from. There's a tendency sometimes to get extra points by showing a team mate one's card.

Students that normally seem too shy to act in front of a group will do so willingly once the stage has been set by the more theatrical in the group and a setting – free of judgments – has been safely established.

Cluck Call

Age Level: any age (6 and up)
Skills/Subject Areas: science, listening skills, cooperative learning
Eco-Concept:
  Adaptation - everything has evolved to fit how and where it lives
Required Materials: blindfolds, rattle
Prep Time: none
Classroom Adaptations/Variations: learn about imprinting in animals and species that imprint on their parents.

Description:

Animal communication is important for a wide range of reasons: to signal the presence of food, to attract a mate, to ward off an intruder, to signal danger or to give reassurance. In many bird species chicks imprint on their mother's call even before they hatch from the egg. By the time chicks hatch out they are so bonded with their mother's "cluck" call that they can locate her even in the midst of other clucking hens.

In this exercise, one person with a strong maternal instinct is chosen to be a grouse (or quail) 'hen' while three to six other players become her clutch of 'chicks'. Have the 'grouse' family spend some time together so the 'hen' can get to distinguish the 'chick's' "peep" sounds. The 'chicks' in turn must learn to distinguish the 'mother hen's' "cluck" calls for reassurance (soft, low clucks) from the alarm calls (fast, high-pitched clucks).

Meanwhile, select a few participants to play the role of predatory rattlesnakes; blindfold them and give them each a small container with beans or pebbles to act as a rattle. The 'chicks' will also be blindfolded for this exercise as they are simulating a situation in which they are away from their mother in tall grass and heavy underbrush.

A beach, meadow, open forest floor, or grassy yard is ideal for this exercise. The instructor sets out the blindfolded 'chicks' throughout the play area and leaves them in a standing position. The 'snakes' are then set out randomly among the 'chicks' and are left lying on their bellies. Everyone else in the group now chooses positions of their own to become obstacles: fallen logs, bushes, boulders or swaying grass between the chick and snake players. Finally, the mother hen is positioned at one extreme end of the playing field where she must stay put, but can oversee all the action.

Instruct all 'chicks' that every time the mother hen gives out the call, "Cluck, cluck," all 'chicks' must respond, "Peep, peep." Instruct the rattlesnake players that every time they're about to strike a 'chick' they must give a short warning with their rattles. Rattlesnake players can only move about crawling on their bellies, while chick players walk upright. The worried 'mother hen' is continually trying to guide her 'chicks' through the underbrush (the maze of players) and the 'snakes' and lead the 'chicks' safely home by alternating alarm calls with reassuring calls.

If the person chosen as the 'hen' has strong maternal instincts she will indeed play a convincing role as the protective mother, and will provide touching moments with those 'chicks' with which she reunites.

Come Back Salmon

Age Level: any age (6 and up)
Skills/Subject Areas: science, problem solving, engaging the senses
Eco-Concepts:

> **Cycles** - Nature works in cycles; the building materials for life must be used over and over again
> **Diversity** - differences in living things allow for the success of all life

Required Materials: a few rolls of blue plastic surveyors tape and film canisters filled with 8-10 fragrances are required to perform this exercise.
Prep Time: high - 30 minutes or more
Classroom Adaptations/Variations: research and report on the life cycle of salmon, discuss the importance of individual behavioral variations in social species.

Description:

Can there be any fish more celebrated for its life cycle than the salmon? From Japan to the Pacific Northwest and much of the North Atlantic, this fish has defined cultures for at least 18,000 years. Salmon have given rise to mythic legends, inspired heraldic crests, and triggered battles for control of rivers and fishing grounds. Because of their staggering abundance, they have also allowed for unprecedented leisure time and rich artistic expression in many aboriginal societies.

Today, many students have a pretty good knowledge of a salmon's lifecycle, thanks to the increasing popularity of Nature documentaries. The route from egg to alevin, smolt to fry, and out to sea is well known. Even more celebrated is the salmon's epic journey from the sea back to the waters where it was born. Like a Greek tragedy, this final act is filled with drama - struggling up insurmountable rapids and falls past a plethora of predators, only to die in its home waters following one passionate act of reproduction.

Just how salmon find their way home after so many years at sea long remained a mystery to science. Only recently was it discovered that the built-in memory of this fish is based on a phenomenal sense of smell. Every waterway has a slightly different chemical composition resulting in a slightly different odor that salmon can detect. Believe it or

47

not, salmon have a sense of smell 100-times better than a dog.

It's hard for us humans, with our limited olfactory sense organ, to fully appreciate a creature that can follow its nose better than a bloodhound on a crime trail, or a pig sniffing out truffles underground. But it is possible, through an experiential exercise - *Come Back Salmon* - to learn how salmon are lured by scents back to their spawning beds.

You will need a few rolls of blue plastic surveyors tape and film canisters filled with 8-10 fragrances to perform this exercise. Oil extracts or artificial flavorings can be purchased in small bottles from the spice section of any supermarket. Commonly available flavorings are: peppermint, lemon, orange, vanilla, banana, coconut, clove, cherry, anise, chocolate, coffee and garlic. It only takes a small cotton swab of these fragrances placed inside plastic film canisters to give you all the scents you need for this exercise. You will need two canisters for each scent, one to set out along the course, and one to have your students sniff at the start of the exercise.

Now set out a watershed course with the blue plastic surveyors tape. It is best to map out your course on paper first so you know exactly how many 'tributaries' you need to have branch off your main 'river' line. If you lay out this 'watercourse' in a forest setting, or branching off from an actual waterway, it will more closely simulate a salmon stream. Be sure to have at least 3-4 'tributaries' branch off your main line, and others that branch off from these, to make the route sufficiently complex and not easy to negotiate.

The object of the *Come Back Salmon* exercise is to have participants, pretending to be salmon, find their way home to their 'spawning grounds' by following 4-5 scent clues in the correct order they were given. Scent canisters attached to trees limbs or rocks at the junction of each 'tributary' must be followed in exactly the right order, or a salmon player will end up at the wrong 'spawning ground'.

It is important to write down the order of smells as they are presented to each player at the start so that the instructor can verify later that each participant actually made it to their correct 'spawning ground'. If you code the cap of the film canisters with a waterproof felt pen it will assist you in keeping track of the sequence of smells each player is presented with. Label PM for peppermint, AN for anise, CO for coconut oil, and so on. Do not, however, let the participants see the codes on the caps or they will have visual clues to follow instead of olfactory ones.

It can take some time for each player to get their set of 4-5 scent clues before they set off on the course, so the instructor may want to enrol some assistants to help speed this along. When all players feel confident that they have sniffed their way to their home stream, go around the course to see which are right and which are wrong.

Bring everyone back together for a group discussion following the exercise. Discuss the fate of those that ended up in the wrong spawning ground. Most will write them off as losers, but are they?

Pose this dilemma to your students. If salmon always return to their home stream to repro-duce, why weren't all the northern stocks from Alaska to Washington State eliminated during the great ice ages? Think about it. All of the coastal rivers were buried under ice - up to a mile deep - for centuries. Logic would dictate that there should be no salmon in these waterways once the ice melted. Salmon should only be found today in the southernmost, un-glaciated watersheds. But the reality is, of course, that every river from Washington State to the Bering Sea supports salmon today. How can this be the case?

The answer to the dilemma is really quite simple. Some salmon have behavior problems - they are like the "un-coachable" kid in the classroom - they don't follow the school. An estimated 2-4% of all salmon go to the wrong stream. Far from being "losers", these deviants re-populated the coast after the ice ages, and it is mostly their offspring, not the offspring of the "normal" salmon, that survive to this day.

Have your students compare this to the emphasis on conformity in human societies. Should we be taking more careful note of Nature's ways?

The Conundrum Hunt

Age Level: any age (6 and up)
Skills/Subject Areas: science, cooperative learning, knowledge of flora and fauna, tuning in to Nature, problem solving
Eco-Concepts:
    Diversity - differences in living things allow for the success of all life
    Interdependence - all things are connected to and depend on other living things
    Community - animals and plants live together in special areas that meet their needs
Required Materials: conundrum list (example pg.51), collecting bag, bug box, paint sample chips
Prep Time: medium- 15-20 minutes students can research and create their own conundrums to challenge classmates or their teacher.

Description:

"This is a conundrum plant," the leader points out as the group follows a trail through the woods. Everyone continues walking and a little farther along, the leader stops the group and points to a different plant. "This is a conundrum plant."

"A what?" asks one of the hikers. "A conundrum plant," the leader reiterates. "But I thought you said that other short plant was a...you-know plant." "You don't have a very good memory," says the leader, and points to a third type of plant. "This is the conundrum." "Hey," say several hikers, "that's a different one." The leader shakes his head and says, "I think we'd better sit down and figure this out."

The leader then points to several plants and trees, asking the name of each one. Some shout out the correct names. Others make wild guesses. "What do the names tell us about these plants? What if I called this one 'Joe' and this one 'Jill'? We know they have different names, that they are different, but we don't know how. If I call this a conundrum plant, all you know is its name, which is easy to forget. You don't know that you can eat the berries or that the leaves stay green all year. It's good to learn the names of plants and animals, but it's more important to learn what makes each one different from the others - how they fit into the forest."

The leader pulls some paper from a pack. "Actually, these are conundrums - questions like riddles that will make you think about the connections between everything here in the forest." The leader hands out the lists. "Once you've figured out the conundrum, you have to search for the object and bring it back."

All that is required to make a conundrum list educational as well as experiential is to use imagination in listing the items everyone will hunt for. For instance, instead of listing "a piece of birch bark," the conundrum list might read "the tree bark that can be used to make baskets, canoes, writing paper, and is a good fire starter." Instead of listing a "sundew plant" in the bog, the list could read "a piece of a plant that eats animals." Conversely, a deer hair or dropping could read "a piece of an animal that eats plants." The important thing here is to require the participants to focus on the relationships between living things more than on the names of the objects they collect. Stress beforehand that only small pieces of plants should be collected, and that the environment where the activity takes place should be damaged as little as possible.

A metamorphic rock could be listed as "a piece of something formed under intense heat and pressure." A dab of mud might be listed as "a piece of something that could turn to shale under intense pressure." One listing that always brings interesting results is "something that has no value in Nature." Many youngsters will bring back dead leaves, twigs or stones for this item. Explain to them how everything in Nature has value.

Conundrum Hunts can be done individually, in pairs or in small groupings. The important thing is not so much what is collected as the process of searching, touching, differentiating and understanding. A list of twelve to twenty objects will keep a group occupied for an hour or more. Small plastic Ziplock bags make good collecting bags, while bug boxes are good additions when insects are involved. Be sure the students release the insects alive and uninjured at the completion of the exercise.

A typical conundrum list might read as follows (correct items are listed in brackets):

- *Something squirrels like to eat (acorns, spruce cones, hazel nuts, mushrooms)*

- *Something small that preys on birds and mammals (mosquito, horse fly, black fly, tick)*

- *A modified scale used for flying (bird feather)*

- *A tree bark natives used for making baskets (cedar, birch, ash)*

- *A bark that breaks off smooth and round like a fish scale (Sitka spruce)*

- *Something that has passed through a digestive tract (any type of animal dropping)*

- *Something sticky that is good for starting fires, healing cuts, and as chewing gum (spruce pitch)*

- *Three different things that convert sunlight to sugar (needles, leaves, moss, ferns)*

- *A plant that fixes nitrogen directly from the air (lichen)*

- *Something that all life requires (water, air, sunlight)*

- *Something that has no value in the forest (litter or something that is not naturally present).*

51

Curious Raccoon Walk

Age Level: any age (6 and up)
Skills/Subject Areas: science, observation skills, knowledge of local flora and fauna, problem solving, cooperative learning

Eco - Concepts:

Energy Flow - the sun is the source of energy for all living things

Cycles - Nature works in cycles; the building materials for life must be used over and over again

Diversity - differences in living things allow for the success of all life

Change - everything is in the process of becoming something else

Interdependence - all things are connected to and depend on other living things

Community - animals and plants live together in special areas that meet their needs

Required Materials: clue cards attached to string, index cards, and pen

Prep Time: high - 30 minutes or more

Description:

Have you ever noticed how exploratory raccoons are when they forage for food? Everything interests them. They want to sniff and touch and taste everything, whether it be up a tree, on the ground, in a burrow, or belly deep in water – nothing stops them. *Curious Raccoon Walk,* strives to bring that same sense of discovery and sensory awareness out in participants.

The best location for this exercise is a natural setting with a variety of habitats: forest, meadow, beach, creek, pond, etc. The more diverse the environment, the richer the experience. Camp staff will need to do some preparation for this exercise by carefully surveying the site for wildlife signs and natural history features. Take along a pen and notepad to record your observations. Examples:

1. tadpoles at pond edge
2. dragonfly over water surface
3. edible blackberries
4. crow's nest in fir tree

5. rabbit droppings
6. squirrel cone cache
7. deer-browsed fern fronds
8. young hemlock trees.

Back in camp the staff can create conundrums on large index cards with waterproof felt pens for each of the observations noted. Examples from above:

1. Now I feed on algae and aquatic plants, later I will attack insects.
2. The male of my species is extremely territorial and will defend his air space.
3. I am a favorite food of black bears and many birds.
4. Look up and see if you can spot my hidden home. I am very protective and aggressive when my young are here.
5. This is all that remains of my last meal. Notice there's no fur, feathers, or bone in my droppings. I am a herbivore.
6. I store my food here for winter use.
7. My tender shoots are high in minerals and vitamins – very important for growing the antlers of the animal that grazes me.
8. You can always identify me by my short, soft needles and drooping top.

Make up fifteen to twenty such cards and number them on the back. Now laminate them in waterproof, clear plastic and attach strings to the top of each sign for hanging.

Return to the area of discovery to set out the signs. Signs for items 1 & 2 can be attached to bobbers directly on the surface of a pond. Set these out deep enough that participants will have to wade in the water up to their knees to read them. If there are any hazards or leeches at such sites, at least the instructor will discover them first.

When the site is completely set up the staff can lead the youngsters there as part of a forest appreciation exercise, or just an outing. Talk about the need to slow down, tune in, and really become part of a place as the best way to discover the wealth of life all around you. "Now, we're all going to become curious like foraging raccoons as we explore this area here," the leader tells the group. "Discover as many things about this

area as possible. There are clues set out to help you in your discoveries, but don't let it end there, find something really amazing you can share with the group when you return."

Participants may set out on this exercise individually or in groups of two. Give each player or team a pen and notepad to record answers to the conundrums and to share their own amazing discoveries.

Encourage everyone to remove their shoes and socks and roll their pants up to their knees before beginning the walk. Explain how curious raccoons like to touch everything, feel their toes squish in the mud as they dig for clams, hunt for frogs, or go to wash their food at a pond's edge. The sensory part of this exercise is as important as the natural history awareness. Let it be a total experience; for many kids it will be their first.

Shoes have replaced bare feet in nearly the entire world today. As a result, few people are in direct touch with the earth, unlike all of our ancestors who walked barefoot for millions of years of human existence. It is important to renew that direct contact – that basic grounded connection. An Elder was once asked what she would do differently if she had her life to live over again. She said, "I'd go barefoot earlier in the spring and later into the fall." She'd probably have enjoyed a *Curious Raccoon Walk*.

Deer Ears

Age Level: any age (6 and up)
Skills/Subject Areas: science, listening skills, tuning in to Nature, knowledge of local flora and fauna, observation
Eco-Concept:
　　Adaptation - everything has evolved to fit how and where it lives
Required Materials: blindfold, scarf, twig 'antlers'
Prep Time: low- less than 10 minutes
Classroom Adaptations/Variations: research unique adaptations of different animals (giraffe, octopus, platypus etc.)

Description:

Choose a quiet forest setting for *Deer Ears,* away from roads, loud creeks or surf, one with plenty of forest litter. "Have you ever wondered why a deer's ears are so big?" the instructor asks.

Have each person cup their hands behind their ears to simulate a deer's. Without changing his or her tone of voice, the instructor asks, "How many think I'm speaking louder now?" The apparent change in volume is fairly dramatic.

"Let's demonstrate just how important a deer's hearing is," the instructor continues. "We're going to play a game called *Deer Ears.* One of you will be blindfolded and will kneel here in the forest like a deer grazing at night. The rest of you will become predators, wolves or cougars. The predators must start the game at least fifteen meters away from the 'deer'. When I give the signal to

start stalking, you must slowly and silently begin pursuing your prey. If the predators get close enough to the 'deer' to snatch a cloth 'tail' from the 'deer's' back pocket, then the 'deer' is dead. But if the 'deer' hears you coming and points in your direction, saying, "Starve!," then you're out of the game."

Now a deer can't be so paranoid that it stops eating and flees with every little movement it hears, or it would probably starve. So to make the situation more realistic the 'deer' will only be able to point and shout, "Starve!" as many times as there are predators (plus two extra).

A staff member will have to monitor the game closely and be certain that all players stop stalking every time the 'deer' says, "Starve!" If the 'deer' points within two or three degrees of a predator, that person is out of the game and must now sit in total silence. (It is best to have each person caught sit quietly beside the instructor.) The instructor can then give the "continue stalking" go-ahead to those predators still in the game.

There is great suspense as the 'wolves' and 'cougars' creep closer to the 'deer'. The successful predators are those who make their advances while the 'deer' is distracted in another direction. The successful 'deer' are constantly alert to sound from any direction, frequently moving their hand-cupped ears in different directions just like real deer, and periodically altering their grazing position. Be sure to keep the 'deer's' ears exposed when tying the blindfold. Small branches resembling deer antlers tied to the head of the 'deer' adds a realistic touch to the game and seems to assist in the role-play.

Let the person who kills the 'deer' become the next 'deer'. This game is so popular with youngsters that everyone in the group will want a turn playing 'deer'. Following the exercise, take a moment to discuss other adaptations deer have to avoid predation, such as long necks, and eyes on the sides of their heads that allow them to see in every direction except right behind them. Speed and agility are other defense strategies. Discuss too the importance of predators keeping deer populations healthy

Digital Decomposition

Age Level: any age (6 and up)
Skills/Subject Areas: science, data recording, observation skills, and technology
Eco-Concepts:

   Cycles - Nature works in cycles; the building materials for life must be used over and over again

   Change - everything is in the process of becoming something else

Required Materials: yarn, sharpened sticks, digital camera and computer, data recording sheet

Prep Time: high - A few hours are needed to set up study plots and download digital photos. A few class periods spread out over 2-3 weeks are required to make and discuss observations.

Description:

Students love to go outdoors and explore; they also love computers and digital cameras. This activity allows them to enjoy both while providing a study focus for exploration and an excuse to go outside often!

The teacher will need to set up and number study plots prior to taking the students outside. The teacher can determine the size of the study plot unless quantitative data will be collected (i.e. how many mushrooms per m2, how much leaf litter per m2). In that case, a 1-meter x 1-meter square is standard.

In the classroom the teacher discusses the activity, places students into groups of 3-4, assigns the groups a study plot and passes out the data sheets to each student. While students are outside they observe, draw and record what they see inside their study plot. The student also takes digital photographs of their study plot for later comparison to the drawings. The outdoor observation is repeated several times (at least 3-4) during the course of a few weeks with new data sheets and photos each time. The end result is a series of photos and drawings that document the change that has taken place during the observation period.

Multiple observations, recording and photographing the study plots allows the students to realize how dynamic Nature is. Nothing remains constant. Hopefully, during the course of the activity new things will grow, ants will build homes, fungus will appear, and the leaf litter will decompose. Witnessing this first hand and recording it with both drawings and digital photos will allow students to make direct connections to their environment. Discussions in the classroom will help students realize that they are part of an ever changing, highly dynamic living world.

Duplication

Age Level: any age (6 and up)
Skills/Subject Areas: science, knowledge of local flora and fauna, relationships in Nature, biodiversity
Eco-Concept:
  Diversity - differences in living things allow for the success of all life
Required Materials: two kerchiefs (or small towels), 12-16 samples from study area
Prep Time: low - less than 10 minutes

Description:

Duplication is an engaging activity that teaches lessons in biological diversity and edible plants. The instructor collects a dozen or more small samples of edible and poisonous plants. With none of the participants watching, the samples are arranged atop a cloth spread on the ground and then hidden beneath a second cloth.

Everyone is now called together and handed their own kerchief. (Sometimes it's nice to do this activity in pairs if the group is large – ten or more).

"Okay, now," the leader begins, "hidden beneath this cloth are a number of different objects that you're going to be able to study for only thirty seconds. Once I cover them over again you'll have three minutes to collect all of the same items from this general area."

The instructor lifts the cover, counts thirty seconds out loud and covers the objects again. While everyone is off looking for the items, the leader calls out the time remaining every thirty seconds. When the three minutes are up, everyone is called together and told to set out their objects atop their kerchiefs.

The instructor pulls out the hidden objects one at a time with some fanfare. "Ta-da! Who's got it and what is it?" the leader asks. Each person who has the same item gives themselves a point. The first person to correctly name the object and tell something about its uses gets a second point. The leader then adds any information she or he can.

It is good to use items such as berries, moss, mushrooms, leaves, etc., to help participants learn of the incredible diversity in an ecosystem. All moss may look the same at first glance, but when closely comparing specimens, there might be a dozen different species collected by a single group.

Duplication, is a popular activity with kids and adults alike. A fruit/nut bar offered as a prize to the individual or team with the highest score acts as further incentive.

Eagle Eyes

Age Level: any age (6 and up)
Skills/Subject Areas: science, math, engaging the senses
Eco-Concept:
  Adaptation - everything has evolved to fit how and where it lives
Required Materials: index card, pen
Prep Time: none
Classroom Adaptations/Variations: learn about birds and mammals with extraordinary vision, or the anatomy and physiology of the eye

Description:

Animals are adapted to meet their special needs in amazing ways. Look at the big radar receptor ears on deer and you know how important hearing is in warning them of approaching danger from a wolf, cougar or other silently stalking predators. Look how large the nose is on a bear compared to its beady, near-sighted eyes and you realize that this is an omnivore, like a pig, heavily dependent on smell to locate carrion, ground tubers, fish and ripe berries. Now consider the size of an eagle's eyes, or other birds of prey that depend on superb vision to find their prey.

Many people think that eagles enlarge images with their eyes, like humans looking through binoculars. This is not actually the case, and would prove quite dangerous to a flying raptor if it were. What allows eagles to spot prey at great distances is not an enlargement of the image but incredible depth perception. A good way to illustrate this for students is to go to a large playing field and stand at one end. Mark a dot on a small index card and hold it up. Have your students face you holding the card while they slowly walk backwards away from it. When they reach the point at which they can no longer see the dot on the card they should stop. This is the farthest point of resolution for their eyes. A group of students might be surprised to see that this distance varies from one person to the next, though there will be a general norm represented by the group standing closest together.

The students are now asked to count their strides back to the instructor and multiply that number by ten. They are then to walk back across the field that combined number of paces and turn around to once again face the index card being held by the teacher. Some students will barely be able to see the card itself from this distance – an eagle, on the other hand, could still make out the dot.

Eagles & Ravens

Age Level: any age (6 and up)
Skills/Subject Areas: P.E., energy burner, team building, knowledge of flora and fauna
Eco-Concepts: (this activity can cover any eco-concepts depending on the nature of the questions asked)
Required Materials: set of true and false questions about Nature
Prep Time: low - less than 10 minutes

Description:

A fast-action contest between two teams, *Eagles and Ravens* demands speed and agility on one hand and quick thinking and intelligence on the other. It's a great physical workout, popular with the participants, and ideal for releasing any pent-up energy.

Divide the group into equal-size teams, distinguished by different colored kerchiefs tied around arms or used as headbands. The Eagle and Raven teams then assemble in two straight lines facing one another, about three to four meters apart. Each team has a 'home free' end zone clearly marked out on the playing field, about twenty to thirty meters behind where they begin. The set-up resembles a small football field, with two end zones and the opposing teams facing each other on opposite sides of the fifty-yard line.

A staff member should have prepared a list of twenty to thirty true and false statements, which will now be presented to the group. If the answer to a statement is "true," the Eagles chase the Ravens. If the answer to the statement is "false," the Ravens chase the Eagles. For every member of the opposing team that is tagged before they reach their end zone, a point is scored for the offensive team. Staff members at each end zone can act as referees to help record tags. Present an equal number of true and false statements to the teams. Sometimes a player shouts out the wrong answer and everyone reacts in error. The instructor can then shout out the correct answer and watch the fun as the pursuers suddenly become the pursued.

This is an ideal way to "test" the participants on the natural history or cultural knowledge they have gained. For instance, natural history statements might be:

1. *Spruce trees are more salt-tolerant than hemlock trees. True. (That is why more spruce than hemlock grows along exposed coasts.)*

2. *Bears eyesight is as good as eagles. False. (Bears are notoriously near-sighted while eagles have vision ten times better than our own.)*

3. *Sundews are plants that eat insects. True. (These insectivorous plants digest flies attracted to their sticky leaves.)*

4. *The sun always sets in the east. False. (It always sets in the west, and depending on the time of year and one's location, it can range from northwest to southwest.)*

5. *True north and magnetic north are often different directions. True. (How much difference depends on where on the Earth you are)*

At the completion of the game the final scores are tallied and the winner declared. Ties do occur, but even a team that wins by a large margin should be encouraged to share any prizes (cookies, apples, etc.) with their distinguished opponents.

Echo Location

Age Level: any age (6 and up)
Skills/Subject Areas: science, P.E., cooperative learning, engaging the senses, listening skills
Eco-Concepts:
>**Interdependence** - all things are connected to and depend on other living things
>**Adaptation** - everything has evolved to fit how and where it lives

Required Materials: blindfolds
Prep Time: none
Classroom Adaptations/Variations: discuss animals which use echo location and discover how it works.

Description:

Echo location is one of the communication marvels of the animal world, and nowhere is it better developed than in whales, dolphins, and bats. "Just think," an instructor says to a group of youngsters eager to play, "all toothed whales can actually 'see' with their ears. Have you ever opened your eyes underwater and discovered how short is the distance you can actually see? Even in clear, shallow water you can't see much further that sixty meters, and at depths of only 400 meters the ocean is pitch black. But water carries sound further and faster than it carries light. Some whales take advantage of this: they have evolved a process called echo location to 'see' with sound.

Sperm whales can find giant squid in total darkness 3.2 kilometers below the surface using echo location. Orca whales can locate huge schools of herring and salmon in the same way, as can dolphins."

"The way it works is pretty neat," the instructor continues enthusiastically.

"To see what lies ahead in the dark ocean, a whale or dolphin sends out a clicking sound. When the click reaches a school of fish or shrimp, it bounces back, like a ball bouncing off a wall. If the click returns quickly to the whale, it knows that the food is close. Besides locating food in this way, whales can also find direction and communicate with one another over incredible distances. Fin whales can send out sounds that can be heard 3,220 kilometers away!"

"Who wants to be a sperm whale hunting for squid in the total dark?" the instructor asks. An eager volunteer is blindfolded. Two or three others are chosen to be 'squid'. All other participants form a big 'ocean' by joining hands in a circle. "Now," the instructor continues, "every time the 'whale' shouts out in a deep voice "Sperm whale!", the 'squid' must immediately respond in a high-pitched voice: "Squid." If the 'whale' should shout "Sperm whale! Sperm whale! Sperm whale!" the 'squid' must mimic with the sonar echo, "Squid, squid, squid."

The 'whale' must capture all 'squid' before he or she can be relieved of 'whale' duties. If two or more blindfolded whales are used for large groups, the instructor must watch the situation carefully and be ready to step in if collisions start to occur. The circle of players defining the boundaries of the game are not idle spectators in this drama. They can decide to put added pressure on the 'squid' by closing the circle tighter and thus making the 'ocean' smaller. This becomes necessary when a slow 'whale' has difficulty.

Any number of variations to this game is possible, such as killer whale/salmon, porpoise/fish, and bat/bugs.

Play this game several times, letting different players take on the predator/prey roles.

Energy Pyramids

Age Level: any age (6 and up)
Skills/Subject Areas: P.E., team building, knowledge of local flora and fauna, relationships in Nature (food webs, symbiosis etc.), problem solving
Eco-Concepts:
   Energy Flow - the sun is the source of energy for all living things
   Interdependence - all things are connected to and depend on other living things
Required Materials: species cards with name or photo of the species
Prep Time: medium- 15-20 minutes
Classroom Adaptations/Variations: challenge the students to design an aquatic and terrestrial energy pyramid in their own bioregion

Description:

Pyramid models are one of the best ways to demonstrate how energy flows through a complex food web or a whole ecosystem. *Energy Pyramids* combines this lesson along with the fun and teamwork of building a hu-

man pyramid. A group of twelve or twenty participants is ideal, as it can be nicely divided into two three-tiered pyramids with six people per group, or two four-tiered pyramids with ten people per group. Extra players can act as team organizers.

To begin, the instructor should show participants a diagram of a food pyramid depicting the various trophic levels – levels of nourishment. (Examples at right)

Green plants are on the bottom at trophic level one, because their energy has been transformed once from the sun to plants. Herbivores (plant eaters) are at trophic level two, because their energy has been transferred twice: from sun to plants and plants to herbivores. Carnivores (meat eaters) that eat herbivores are at trophic level three, because their energy has been transferred three times: from sun to plants, plants to herbivores, and herbivores to carnivores. High-level carnivores (those that eat other carnivores) are trophic level four because their energy has been tranfered four times.

Once the participants understand the principle of energy transfer, the instructor should explain that this is a very simple model. "It is possible to have many more levels of a pyramid," the instructor points out. "For instance, it takes a lot of sunlight to grow single-celled sea plants, which provide food for microscopic sea animals, which feed needlefish, which in turn feed herring, which feed salmon, which ultimately feed a bear, eagle, killer whale, or human. We are going to look at three or four levels of that energy transfer in a pyramid building contest."

Each team is now presented with a set of large index cards with animals or plants showing a particular energy flow printed boldly and illustrated on each. The object of the game is to see which team can build their pyramid and label each level first. Only correct labeling counts, so careful thought is as important to success as speed is.

The index cards can be strung to hang behind the neck of one player at each level, or, alternatively, they can simply be held in the mouth. The two teams build their pyramids

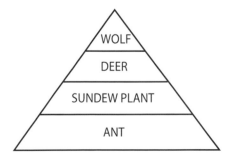

directly facing one another so they are constantly aware of the other's progress as well as any errors in their logic.

The first team to have all their members in position with the correct labeling wins the set. Following the inevitable collapse of the pyramid, it is time to start over, with each team given a new set of cards. Five to six sets are usually sufficient to exhaust almost everyone.

A short discussion should follow each pyramid-building session to be certain all players understood why the energy transfers worked the way it did. An interesting addition to this game is to give four colored tennis balls to the bottom players in each pyramid. "These are pesticide balls," the instructor points out. "You must pass them up to each level above you, and the top-level predator must hold all four because that's where they end up in the real food pyramid. In a real world three-level food chain, the predator would get 111 'balls' because each lower trophic level is ten times larger than the one above."

Try another pyramid where the instructor says, "I wonder what would happen if we pulled out part of a level?" and proceeds to do so. "So what happens when the herring or shrimp get over fished? If oil spills kill the plankton? Or too many high-level carnivores are exterminated?"

Be sure to choose a good location for this activity like a sandy beach, soft grassy meadow, or mossy forest floor, and carefully monitor the event to prevent any injuries. Older participants should not climb upon one another, but merely lean onto those below them (Example below)

Follow that Pheromone

Age Level: any age
Skills/Subject Areas: science, observation
Eco-Concept:
  Adaptation - everything has evolved
  to fit how and where it lives
Required Materials: spice oils
Prep Time: none
Classroom Adaptations/Variations:
complete a study on ants, insects, or insect
body parts before going outside to familiar-
ize students with ants and associated ter-
minology

Description:

Have you ever wondered why individual ants you see follow a straight line? They never seem to get distracted or lose the trail that leads to food or shelter. It seems almost like magic since there is nothing visible that they are following.

It's not magic at all! In fact you can do a simple activity to explain how they find their way!

Ants communicate via chemical signals called pheromones. Pheromones help insects find everything from a mate to a trail that has been marked in order for other insects of the same species to follow.

In the case of the mysterious ant line you might see crossing a forest trail there is an invisible path of pheromones that the ants are following. The pheromones help other ants 'sense' the path that they should fol-

low. As long as they stay on the pheromone path they will continue to march single file to their destination.

You can prove this to yourself with a simple experiment. Since the pheromones are chemicals they can be erased! All you need to do is wipe your finger across the ant line and see what happens!

The oils and moisture in your hand will wipe away the pheromone signal. This will cause temporary chaos for the ants. You'll notice that they seem to lose their way! Their per-fect marching line has been disrupted, at least until they can re-establish their trail by marking it with more pheromones.

Try it next time your class stumbles across an ant line out on the trail, in the school park-ing lot, sidewalk, or even in your classroom. Be careful not to get bitten by the ants.

So that students can see how this works follow this simple plan. Obtain a few spice extracts from a supermarket and dabble three different scented trails across a lawn. (Peppermint, anise, and garlic oils work well for this). Next divide your group into three 'ant colonies' and dab a bit of each scent on each participants' wrist to designate the 'pheromone' for each 'colony'.

Now, send the three groups of 'ants' out to crawl across the lawn to find their 'phero-mone' trail and follow it. (It can lead to a prize hidden in the bushes or behind a rock).

As an added challenge, blindfold students and ask them to try again!

Food Chain Chase

Age Level: any age
Skills/Subject Areas: science, P.E., math
Eco-Concepts:
    Energy Flow - the sun is the source of energy for all living things
    Interdependence - all things are connected to and depend on other living things
    Community - animals and plants live together in special areas that meet their needs
Required Materials: dead leaves to serve as 'food' for the 'insect larvae', tags to label each participant as a 'critter' in the food chain, poster paper and markers to graph animal populations
Time Commitment: 20-30 minutes

Description:

Designate the playing field by setting boundaries and telling students where they can run and play. While showing the boundaries, spread the dead leaves you have previously collected throughout the area. Students that are 'insect larvae' will have to collect these later as food.

To play the game students must be briefed on what eats what in an aquatic ecosystem (i.e. mayfly and caddis fly larvae feed on various plants, dragonfly larvae prey on small fish and even each other, small fish eat various insect larvae, large fish eat small fish, and birds can eat large and small fish).

Next, the students are allocated roles of plant, insect, fish or bird. The 'plants' are the 'home base' for the 'larvae'. The 'larvae' can't be eaten by a predator while in the shelter of a plant. However, students cannot hide and sit on the plant all day! They must go out and search for food. The 'insects' can only seek the protection of a 'plant' for 10 seconds before having to run back out and collect a designated number of dead leaves that serve as food. 'Plants' are responsible for keeping track of time. Their job is to push the 'insects' into the playing field after 10 seconds.

When the 'caddisflies' and 'mayflies' venture out they might be eaten by a 'dragonfly larvae' or 'small fish'. Meanwhile, the 'dragonflies' must avoid being eaten by the 'small fish' while they look for food. The 'big fish' must avoid being eaten by the 'bird(s)' while they search for food. When a critter is "eaten" (tagged) it is then "turned" into whatever eats it (this simulates reproduction). For example, if a 'small fish' is eaten by a 'large fish' then the 'small fish' becomes a 'large fish' that chases 'small fish'! Pretty soon chaotic fun emerges as students chase and try to "feed" on each other while avoiding being eaten themselves!

To avoid the game from being over run by 'birds' (or any other top predator), the instructor can get involved by ensuring that the 'birds' eventually die from old age and are converted into various other critters through the process of decay and renewal. To do this the instructor may shout to a 'bird', "You've died of old age. To balance the ecosystem, you've been changed into a small fish!"

Discuss how this really happens in Nature and how everything is in a constant process of renewal.

Variations: Introduce an herbicide that kills half the plants and see what happens to the insect larvae and fish populations. Discuss how herbicides can have repercussions throughout the food chain. Introduce an insecticide that kills most of the insect larvae. See what happens to the fish and bird populations.

Introduce humans which over fish the area. Discuss wise use of resources and how we can impact an environment

Keep track of and graph the results of different populations (and the effects of the introduction of different variables on these populations) throughout several rounds of play.

Start the game with different numbers of plants, insects, fish and birds (i.e. play one game with lots of 'plants' and another with few 'plants', play one game with a lot of 'birds' and another with few 'birds'). Discuss how these variations in populations affect other populations.

Forest Fragrances

Age Level: any age (6 and up)
Skills/Subject Areas: science, arts, observation, cooperative learning, self expression, tuning in to Nature, engaging the senses, sampling
Eco-Concept:
  Diversity - differences in living things allow for the success of all life
Required Materials: clear plastic cups
Prep Time: none

Description:

"Take time to stop and smell the roses," we are reminded from time to time in our increasingly frantic, urban lifestyles. But how many of us ever actually do this? We spray deodorizing chemicals with names like 'pine mist', 'forest bouquet' and 'cedar spice' in our bathrooms, and hang air fresheners in our cars with equally fanciful names, but how many of us have ever taken the time to get a whiff of real forest fragrances? This simple activity allows participants to do just that.

Find a good forest location without a lot of dense under brush, but with good botanical diversity for this exercise. Give each of the participants a clear plastic glass and instruct them to collect small samples of objects from the surrounding forest with pleasing aromas to them. Girls can be given the task of developing a new perfume line, while boys set out to discover cologne, to supply the growing demand for natural Earth products.

Challenge the students to come up with a name for the new fragrance line they are developing, and encourage them to artistically arrange the forest items they put in their glass, for this will be the new promotional image for their fragrance.

This exercise is best done individually as no two people share the same sense of smell. Allow ample time for exploration as the students sniff their way through forest litter, flowers, moldy leaves, spruce and pine needles, cedar fronds, mushrooms, rotting wood, tree saps and pine pitch, berries, and even aromatic insects. If there are any endangered plants in the vicinity, be sure to point them out to the students and request that they not disturb them by taking samples.

After 20-30 minutes, call everyone back together into a circle and select one participant - who believes they have a superior sense of smell - to be the judge of the various entries. Blindfold that person to ensure 'blind justice' and start passing the forest fragrance glasses around the circle for all to enjoy. The students will be amazed how no two glasses containing fragrances smell alike.

As each entry is carefully passed to the 'judge,' assign it a number. The blindfolded 'judge' must remember the number associated with each fragrance in case they need to recall it for another sniff, as well as to declare the winning entry. Once the best aromas are selected in the two categories - - girls 'perfume' and boy's 'cologne' - remove the blindfold from the 'judge' and let that person now select the best arrangement, and the best name for their product.

This is a popular activity for groups of all ages, but a lot more environmental awareness can be built into the exercise that merely tuning in to Nature's amazing fragrance line. "Why do things smell differently?" you might ask your group. "Why do most flowers and berries smell sweet, and mushrooms smell musky, but spruce, pine, fir and cedar smell pungent?" Discuss the importance of plant scents in attracting pollinators, birds and mammals necessary to disperse their seeds, or acting as natural insecticides to deter predators.

Greet - a - Tree

Age Level: any age (6 and up)
Skills/Subject Areas: science, observation, engaging the senses, tuning in to Nature, cooperative learning, problem solving
Eco-Concept:
    Diversity - differences in living things allow for the success of all life
Required Materials: blindfolds
Prep Time: none

Description:

"Which two people in our group look the most alike?" the hike leader suddenly asks, as a group of youngsters stop to rest in the forest. There is a lot of looking back and forth before everyone realizes there really aren't many similarities. "Well, no two trees in the forest look any more alike than any two individuals in your group," the leader proclaims. "Let's have a look." Take some time to compare differences in bark texture, girth, trunk configuration, height and limb structure, even between trees of the same species. Now have the group divide into pairs, and, while one in each party is being blindfolded with a kerchief, the instructor comments:

"There is a tree in this forest that has been waiting to meet you all its life,and it is much older than you. The tree is a little shy about this first encounter," the guide explains, "so we are having your friend lead you there blindfolded. When you greet your tree for the first time, touch it gently. Feel how strong it is. Touch its bark and limbs. See if you can wrap your arms around its trunk. Get to know your tree as best you can, because you will need to find each other later."

The participants set off in pairs. The guide for each blindfolded youngster should hold one of his or her partner's hands extended out in front and have the other hand reassuringly rested on the partner's shoulder. Youngsters love this part of the exercise, though there can be a tendency to abuse the privilege by leading the blindfolded into a lot of unnecessary obstacles. Remind everyone that they will be exchanging positions at some point, so they will want to do unto their partners as they would have their partners do unto them.

Once the blindfolded participants have had some time alone with their trees and comes to know them well by touch, they are then led (rather indirectly) back to the place from which they started. The blindfolds are removed, and the youngsters are asked to find and greet their trees again.

Most participants will be able to locate their trees from memory, but occasionally some become extremely disoriented and search in vain. Have their partners give them clues such as "you're getting warmer (colder)" until they and their trees are successfully reunited.

Some youngsters become so attached to their trees that they seek them out again and again during the course of a program. A distressed camper that runs off to be alone for some particular reason can often be found at the base of his or her tree.

do," the leader answers, "but their ears are hidden behind a face full of feathers. An owl's ears extend along the skull from the top of the head to well below the beak. It's almost as if their face were one big radar receptor dish that can detect subtle sound from the tiniest movement."

Hoo Hoo Hoot Owl

Age Level: any age (6 and up)
Skills/Subject Areas: science, listening skills, relationships in Nature, problem solving, engaging the senses
   Eco-Concepts:
   Interdependence - all things are connected to and depend on other living things
   Adaptation - everything has evolved to fit how and where it lives
Required Materials: blindfolds, peanuts in the shell
Prep Time: low - less than 10 minutes
Classroom Adaptations/Variations:
   research and discuss the anatomy and physiology of an owls head, especially their hearing. How does their head bobbing behavior help pinpoint prey?

Description:

A leader has brought a small group of campers to a forest clearing as dusk approaches. Discussions center around the animals of the night that are starting to become active: bats and moths, raccoons and frogs, mice and owls, etc.

"How do you suppose an owl sitting atop one of these trees in the dark of night can detect a mouse hidden in the grass and ferns?" the leader asks. "They have good night vision," someone contributes. "That's true," the leader responds, "but more importantly they have the most awesome sense of hearing." "But they don't have big ears like a deer," a kid protests. "Actually they

"Let's experience this for ourselves," the leader continues. "Who wants to be an owl?" One or two participants are selected as 'owls,' and blindfolded so they must rely totally on hearing to catch their prey. (Remember to leave the ears of the owl players unobstructed when tying the blindfolds.) All other participants will play the role of mice foraging for food.

The instructor sets out eight to ten feeding stations for the 'mice', small piles of peanuts in the shell. One station is set out for each mouse player, but each player is only allowed to eat one peanut per station before they must crawl on to the next.

The 'owls', once blindfolded, are set out amongst the foraging 'mice'. The 'owls' can cup their hands behind their ears for better hearing as they try to pick up the sounds of feeding or moving 'mice'. If an 'owl' detects a sound, points in that direction and says, "Hoo! Hoo!" then any 'mouse' that has been caught in that position is "dead" or out of the game. The 'owl' is then moved by the leader to the spot where that 'mouse' was captured.

Because the 'owl' (or owls) are almost always changing locations, even the most distant (feeding or moving) 'mouse' is never safe from detection. This exercise is especially entertaining if it is done when the kids are quite hungry between mealtimes.

The object of the game for the 'mice' is to stay alive as long as possible, eating as much as possible. When all mice players have been caught, the remaining peanuts are rewards for the successful 'owls'.

Hungry, Hungry Marten

Age Level: any age (6 and up)
Skills/Subject Areas: P.E, science, energy burner, cooperative learning, team building, relationships in Nature
   Eco-Concepts:
   Interdependence - all things are connected to and depend on other living things
   Adaptation - everything has evolved to fit how and where it lives
Required Materials: scarves or arm bands to distinguish the 'martens'
Prep Time: none
Classroom Adaptations/Variations: research other predatory species and determine their home range in relation to their prey population density

Description:

In a forest setting, ask the group to name as many animals as they can that live in the temperate forests: bear, deer, raccoon, squirrel, toad, woodpecker, thrush, mouse, shrew, weasel, marten, etc. Discuss how the forest provides food and shelter for these species, and the range of territory each might hold within the forest. For instance, the home range of the marten is largely determined by food availability. A few square kilometers may be sufficient in times of abundance, but up to thirty-eight square kilometers will be required in times of scarcity. Red squirrels are an important part of a marten's diet, but their home range is much smaller. A marten can do everything a squirrel can do – climb trees, and leap from branch to branch with great speed and agility.

The advantage the squirrel has in escaping the marten is that it knows its home range better. Squirrels have highways in the tree-tops and on the ground that they know by heart; they also have refuge holes inside trees, holes too small for the marten to enter.

Choose one volunteer to be a 'marten'. (Two 'marten' should be chosen if the group is large-more than six to nine.) All other players become 'squirrels'. The 'squirrels' have one tree in the forest that provides marten-proof shelter. If they can reach this tree and shout "Hungry, Hungry Marten" before a 'marten' tags them, then they are home free. The game begins with the 'squirrels' out gathering cones some distance away from their refuge tree. Suddenly, the instructor shouts, "There's a 'marten' on the hunt!" All 'squirrels' scatter. The 'marten' can position themselves within ten meters of the refuge tree during the game, but unless they pursue some 'squirrels' for a meal they will surely go hungry. The 'squirrel' family will discover that the best strategy for getting home free is to combine a lot of squirrel chatter with a lot of fast movement to distract and confuse the 'marten'.

This game can be played several different ways. The object of one version is to get as many squirrels as possible (preferably all) to the home tree. 'Squirrels' that are tagged out before they can reach the tree must sit around the base of the tree. Those that reach the tree safely can stand up touching the tree. All can shout encouragement to those still trying to get 'home' safely. Any time both a male and female squirrel player reaches the tree safely, "reproduction" is declared and all squirrel players are once again alive and free-much to the dismay of the 'marten'. In a second version, even faster paced, each time a 'squirrel' safely reaches the tree and shouts "Hungry, Hungry Marten," he or she immediately becomes the new 'marten' and the former 'marten' becomes a 'squirrel'.

Speed, agility, camouflage, and surprise are all key element in the strategies of both squirrel and marten. Expect to be winded after this game. While everyone catches their breath, the instructor should point out that only a century ago the marten was quite common throughout the extensive forests of North America. He or she asks, "How many of you have seen a marten?" Most likely no one in the group has ever spotted a marten.

Today the species is one of the rarest predators in North America because so much of its forest habitat has been lost. In the past few decades, one-half of all the old-growth temperate forests on the planet have been cut. "What does that mean to animals like the marten and countless others?" the instructor asks. "In saving parks and wild areas, how much is enough? Would a twenty-square-kilometre forest preserve protect squirrels? Would it protect martens? Remember, if one marten, in times of scarcity, requires up to thirty-eight square kilometers, and it takes two martens to reproduce, then we need a much larger area. An even larger area will be required to protect a healthy population with genetic diversity. Maintaining the biological diversity – the great complexity of animals and plants of this planet, will be one of the greatest challenges your generation will face."

Imagine Leaf

Age Level: any age (6 and up)
Skills/Subject Areas: arts, science, observation, knowledge of flora and fauna, self expression, tuning in to Nature,
Eco-Concept:
   Diversity - differences in living things allow for the success of all life
Required Materials: index card, pen or pencil
Prep Time: none
Classroom Adaptations/Variations: look for your imagine leaf in a botany book or on the Internet

Description:

Nature is diverse, almost beyond imagining. This is especially true in the equatorial tropics. A temperate forest might be considered exceptionally rich to have 20 tree species growing over a vast area. A tropical forest, by comparison, can boast up to 200 tree species in a single hectare.

Imagine Leaf is a simple but effective exercise that illustrates Nature's phenomenal diversity. It is a more profound exercise when conducted on a hike through a tropical rainforest where biodiversity is at its greatest, but it is also possible to enjoy this activity in a neighborhood park or forest most anywhere in the world.

Start by handing out small (pocket–sized) index cards to all participants and ask them to draw the wildest, most bizarre leaf shape they can possibly imagine. Once they have completed this task have them sign their name to their masterpiece, then set off on a hike into the forest.

"You know what?" the instructor can say to the students once they enter the cool shade of the forest, "Mother Nature already had the same idea as you. Your imaginary leaf is no fantasy at all, it already exists somewhere in this forest."

"No way," someone will undoubtedly object, "I drew a Mickey Mouse face on my leaf; I'll never find that."

"Then you'll just need to look even more closely," the leader instructs.

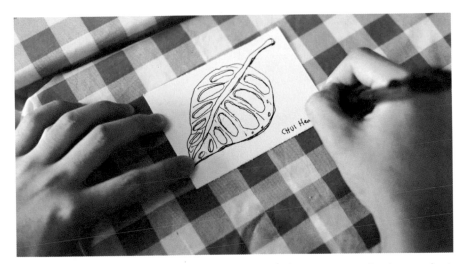

Leaves not only display infinite diversity in size, shape and texture between different species, but no two leaves on a single plant are the same. Insect damage, molds, lichens and algae growth can colonize the surface of mature leaves with the most unusual patterns. These external growths, called epiphilae, lend the army camouflage patterns to the surface of many tropical rainforest leaves. In a setting like this, it is no great challenge to find a leaf resembling a Mickey Mouse face.

Once everyone has had a chance to find the leaf that most closely resembles their drawing, it's time to judge the results. Lay out all of the index cards on a table back in the classroom with the leaves beside them for all to see. Let the students themselves be the judges of the closest match. Now challenge them to identify the leaf they selected. Few will be able to do this so it is

best to have resource books on plant identification available.

It is ironic how few species of plants contemporary students can correctly name, but how many corporate logos they instantly recognize, even from a distance. Help them see for themselves that this is not for lack of mental ability, it's rather a lack of outdoor experience and a good mentor.

On a piece of paper challenge your students to draw and identify the leaf shapes of 10 tree species. On the reverse side of the paper have them draw and identify 10 corporate logos. Compare the results.

If you're still not convinced of the need to further environmental education in the school curriculum, this last exercise might help persuade you.

Impulse

Age Level: any age (6 and up)
Skills/Subject Areas: science, team building, cooperative learning
Eco-Concept:
  Adaptation - everything has evolved to fit how and where it lives
Required Materials: coin to flip, an object to grab (a plastic or stuffed animal/fish)
Prep Time: low - less than 10 minutes

Description:

This is a good companion activity to *Eagle Eyes* (page 58.)

Eagles not only depend on superb vision, but lightening fast reflexes when seizing prey on the wing – a fish snatched from the surface of the water, or a rabbit or ground squirrel darting through the grass. To help the students understand the importance of quick eye-to-claw motor control, have them form two lines, holding hands, with equal numbers of players facing each other no more than two meters apart. At one end of the line up the first students on each team will become the 'eagle's eye'. At the other end of the line ups, the last student on each team will become the 'eagle's claw'. All the students in the middle will become the nerve connection signaling messages from the eye to the claw.

Two simple props are all that's required for this exercise – a coin and a cut-out (or stuffed animal) of a rabbit, ground squirrel, or fish. The food prop is set on the ground exactly half-way between the 'claw' students at the far end of the line. Everyone has their eyes closed throughout each round of play, except for the eagle eye players at the head of the line. Each time the instructor flips a coin in front of the eye players and it comes up 'heads', they are to instantly squeeze the hand of the person beside them. The hand squeeze is then transferred quietly but quickly down the line of players to the 'claw'. Once a claw player feels the squeeze they can open their eyes to snatch the food prop.

The team that is first to grab the food prop wins that round of play, and rotates one position so that the 'claw' person now goes to the head of the line to become the new 'eagle eye'. The game ends when all of the players on a team have had a turn in the 'eye' position. A team that tries to cheat, or reacts wrongly to the coin toss, has to shift one position in the opposite direction, so that the eye player now returns to the position of claw player.

Along with these exercises it is good to get the students sitting in the shade of a tree, or somewhere else outdoors that's comfortable for a general discussion on:

- the role eagles play as top level predators maintaining healthy populations of their prey species

- effects of human developments on habitat requirements for eagles

- DDT contamination in the environment and its impact on eagle reproduction

- the power of the eagle as an image used in ancient heraldic crests and as symbols for modern nation states

Junior Naturalist

Age Level: any age (6 and up)
Skills/Subject Areas: peer teaching, science, knowledge of flora and fauna, speaking skills, listening skills, self expression, self knowledge
Eco-Concepts: (dependent on what is on the trail and the concepts the teacher emphasizes)

> **Energy Flow** - the sun is the source of energy for all living things
> **Cycles** - Nature works in cycles; the building materials for life must be used over and over again
> **Diversity** - differences in living things allow for the success of all life
> **Change** - everything is in the process of becoming something else
> **Interdependence** - all things are connected to and depend on other living things
> **Community** - animals and plants live together in special areas that meet their needs
> **Adaptation** - everything has evolved to fit how and where it lives

Materials Required: none
Prep Time: none

Description:

Students get to share their knowledge and teach their peers during this game. To set the stage for the game it is best to put elemtary-aged students in pairs. This helps them to overcome shyness and help each other remember the lesson they will teach their peers. For older students it may not be necessary to work in pairs.

To get started take the first pair of students to a special spot (i.e. a rotting stump). Tell the students what makes their spot special (i.e. the stump is decomposing and turning into soil which will feed future plants). Tell them that they will teach everyone that passes by their spot what they just learned!

Send the second pair of students to the meet the first pair. As they arrive they say "Hey, Naturalist! Teach me about this special spot!" After they have learned the value of that special spot (that rotting stumps turn into food for future plants) then they will be sent to their own location (i.e. a patch of lichen). The teacher then communicates the value of that special spot (i.e. that a lichen is a symbiotic relationship between a fungus and an algae. The fungus provides the

algae with a place to live and in return the algae use photosynthesis to provide food for the fungus). Then the third pair of students goes to meet the first pair to learn about the rotting stump and the second pair to learn about the lichen. They are then sent to their own special spot to become Junior Naturalists.

This process is repeated until all the students have been to all the special spots and learned what makes them special.

As you can see everything you find in the forest, in a field or outdoors can be a special spot. Examples:

A rotting stump - the stump is decomposing and turning into soil which will feed future plants. It may also be a habitat for beetles, termites, spiders, ants and other critters.

A lichen - lichens are interesting in that they feel velvety smooth. They are also special because they are a great example of a special type of symbiosis known as mutualism in which both species benefit from living together closely. The fungus provides a base for the algae to live in (which they can't get on their own) while the algae provide food for the fungus since they can photosynthesize and fungi can't! A great way to remember this is to tell the

kids, "Freddy Fungus took a likin' (lichen) to Alice Algae and they got married and lived happily ever after!"

A leaf - living leaves are carrying out a pretty amazing feets of capturing light and converting it to sugars. Dead leaves are returning their nutrients to the soil through decomposition. You can also engage the sense by examining the texture, shape, smell and color or different leaves. (See the *Imagine Leaf* activity pg.74)

Tree bark - tree bark demonstrates an amazing array of textures and odors for students to explore. From the muscle smooth bark of Iron Wood, the sweet vanilla smell of a Ponderosa Pine, the twisted red branches of Manzanita and the paper like bark of the Birch – tree bark is fascinating to explore!

A rock - rocks are constantly leeching minerals into the soil through erosion by wind and water. There minerals are crucial to the health of the plants that use them and the animals that feed on the plants.

A piece of litter - a piece of trash found in a place of beauty can be a perfect learning moment for a students to connect the value of keeping our environment clean and how their individual actions can lead to achieving this goal!

Mystery Critter

Age Level: any age (6 and up)
Skills/Subject Areas: science, knowledge of flora and fauna, problem solving co-operative learning
Eco-Concepts:

> **Diversity** - differences in living things allow for the success of all life
> **Interdependence** - all things are connected to and depend on other living things
> **Community** - animals and plants live together in special areas that meet their needs
> **Adaptation** - everything has evolved to fit how and where it lives

Required Materials: index cards with clues (see examples pgs.80-81), container with paper and pens for making guesses, award or prize (optional)
Prep Time: high – 30 minutes or more
Classroom Adaptations/Variations: challenge students to come up with a series of 6-8 clues for a species to test their classmates (and teacher)

Description:

Everyone loves the fun of a guessing game, and this activity has been known to absorb both students and adults almost to the point of obsession. *Mystery Critter* introduces students to specific characteristics of a species, and animal behavior traits, in a way they are likely to never forget.

The object of the exercise is simply to guess the species that a clue is given for at the start or end of each class session, or at each mealtime in a camp setting. The clues are read out loud and posted on a wall. Nearby is a canister labeled "Mystery Critter" with a slit in the lid, pens and small pieces of paper for the participants to record their guesses, along with the name of the student making the guess. Players need to be reminded that only the first correct answer drawn from the canister is the winner, so it does not favor a person to be shouting out what they believe the answer to be. Each player is only allowed one new guess for each new clue. Both plants and animals can be used in this exercise, and it is good to draw examples from local ecosystems whenever possible.

Clues should start out very general and progress in an order that keeps the guessing going as long as possible. For instance, a first days clue might read: "I am found on every continent." Six days later, if no one has yet guessed correctly, the clue for the same species might read more specifically: "I leave a scent trail for others of my kind to follow." At this point there should be many correct answers in the canister – an ant!

It's fun randomly drawing and reading each of the guesses aloud, and the name of the person that made the guess. "That's absolutely right, John," the leader might reply to a student's guess, "but it's not the species we're looking for." Everyone keeps trying until a winner is found. Chocolate bars, or a certificate for a chore-free day, are huge incentive prizes in a camp. Teachers in a classroom setting can easily think of other forms of reward. Very often, just the public recognition of getting the right answer is reward enough.

It's a fun challenge to research your own species and make up a series of your own clues, but here's a few to get you started:

1) I can fit through an opening the size of my mouth, or larger.
2) I always return to my home to eat.
3) I am very tidy and always clean up after every meal.
4) I have a beak!
5) I am remarkably intelligent and can solve complex problems.
6) I express my emotions by changing colors.
7) When frightened, I can disappear in a cloud of ink.
(Answer: OCTOPUS)

1) I can live to be 9,000 years old, one of the oldest living things on Earth.
2) I was used to date the stone sculptures on Easter Island.
3) The ancient Egyptians stuffed their mummies with me.
4) Less than half the species of me recorded in California in 1900 exist today.
5) I absorb my food directly from the air.
6) I am the favorite food of caribou.
7) I colonize bare rock surfaces and act as a foothold for other plants.
8) I am not one, but a partnership between two living things (algae & fungus).
(Answer: LICHEN)

1) The male of my species is extremely territorial.
2) I am never found far from fresh water.
3) I prey on stickleback fish, but only as a juvenile.
4) Most of my life is lived under water.
5) My ancestors were much bigger in the time of the dinosaurs.
6) Females of my species deposit their eggs on the surface of ponds.
7) I can hover in flight like a hummingbird.
   (Answer: DRAGONFLY)

1) I can find my way hundreds of kilometers back to the place I was born.
2) I can live for 30-years.
3) I nurse my babies.
4) The female of my species mates early in the fall, but keeps the sperm alive in her body for 8-months before fertilization occurs in the spring.
5) When I'm hunting, I catch and consume my prey every 7-seconds.
6) I belong to the most successful species of mammals – 20% of all mammals on Earth.
7) I spend the winter in a cave hibernating.
8) I am the only mammal that truly flies.
   (Answer: LITTLE BROWN BAT)

1) I can accelerate fifty times faster than the space shuttle!
2) I can survive months without feeding.
3) I can withstand enormous pressure.
4) I can remain frozen for more than a year, and then revive!
5) I have claimed more human victims than all the wars ever fought.
6) I can jump 150-times my own length, either vertically or horizontally.
7) I am not a dogs best friend.
   (Answer: FLEA)

1) I tirelessly track my prey.
2) I have been around for 50 million years.
3) I can consume two and a half times my body weight when I feed.
4) There are more than 3,000 species of me.

5) I am found in the greatest numbers in the arctic and sub arctic.
6) Most of my species are found in the canopy of tropical rainforests.
7) I am very attracted to carbon dioxide emissions.
8) The female of my species is the blood thirsty one.
   (Answer: MOSQUITO)

1) I am found on every continent.
2) There are more than 1,000 different species of me.
3) When I wake up in the morning, I stretch, I yawn, and I wash myself just like humans.
4) My home range can be greater than that of a lion pride.
5) I am incredibly strong and can carry an object ten times my body weight.
6) Some of my kind milk aphids like cows, others grow fungus on leaf cuttings.
7) I make up the greatest biomass (weight of living matter) of any species on Earth.
8) I leave a scent trail for others of my kind to follow.
   (Answer: ANT)

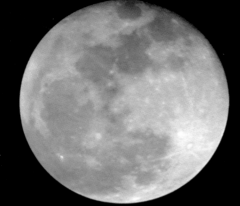

Night Safari

Age Level: any age (6 and up)
Skills/Subject Areas: science, tuning in to Nature, knowledge of local flora and fauna, relationships in Nature, observation, peer teaching, cooperative learning, engaging the senses
Eco-Concepts:

Diversity - differences in living things allow for the success of all life
Interdependence - all things are connected to and depend on other living things
Community - animals and plants live together in special areas that meet their needs
Adaptation - everything has evolved to fit how and where it lives

Required Materials: charcoal or black face paint, penlight for each student
Prep Time: none
Classroom Adaptations/Variations: research local nocturnal animals in your area before or after going outside to see them

Description:

Few youngsters realize that as many creatures inhabit the world of darkness as inhabit the daylight. *Night Safari* is an adventure into the little-explored shady side of the Earth.

To prepare for *Night Safari,* blacken everyone's hands and faces with burnt cork. All explorers should wear dark clothing, long-sleeved shirts, and long pants. (Try not to use insect repellent.) Rub fir branches on the back of the neck and over one's clothing to help disguise human scent. It won't take long before the campers get excited about the prospect of wildlife sightings in the dark, and fully understand the need for camouflage.

Set the mood for the evening by talking in a hushed voice about some of the nocturnal wildlife the group might encounter: deer, raccoons, mice, skunks, bats, owls, rabbits, coyotes. The possibilities, of course, will vary with each area. The forest provides an ideal setting for a *Night Safari* because of the intensified darkness, but desert, tundra, and wild meadows are also suitable during the dark phases of the moon.

Take a bright flashlight on the safari only for emergencies. Let the group learn to improve their night vision, entering the forest just as darkness fully descends, and slowly adjusting to the reduced light. Total darkness does not fully exist even in the deep gloom of the forest at night. Have everyone look up to realize that they can still draw the outline of the treetops against the sky with their fingertips.

Now have the participants move as far away from the instructor as they feel comfortable. Explain that the best chance of viewing night creatures will come to those who remain perfectly still, and that the further spread out the group becomes, the better opportunities for sightings. Everyone must understand that any unnecessary movement or noise will spoil the experience for the entire group.

The instructor should choose a location animals are known to frequent, such as a natural salt lick, watering hole, deer trail, grazing location, den site, or owl tree. If the participants become impatient and appear fidgety after a while (fifteen to twenty minutes), light a candle as the signal for them to all come back together. Have everyone share their secret sightings in a soft whisper. Ask if anyone felt fearful or even uncomfortable being in the dark alone. Ask too if anyone overcame some of their fear of the dark during the exercise.

Even if no wildlife sightings turned up during the solo session, the next activity will surely uncover some. Turn everyone's attention to the little creatures of the night, the mice, shrews, frogs, and others who have evolved abilities to locate their prey, avoid predation, or attract a mate in the dark: the bat's sonar; the owl and deer's superb hear-

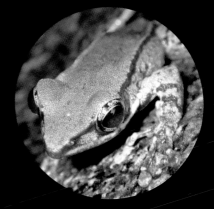

ing; the frog's, cricket's, and katydid's singing; and the firefly's illumination. "Let's become one of those creatures, while we explore," the instructor says excitedly. Tiny penlights are handed out to all the participants. "You are all fireflies," the guide tells the group. "Spread out wherever you like and use your light to explore for life in the dark. If you discover something interesting you want to share with others, don't speak, just blink your light on and off, like a firefly, as a signal for them to come to you."

This is an absorbing activity that can go on late into the night. If the sky is clear and there is a clearing nearby, stargazing makes a perfect close to the *Night Safari*.

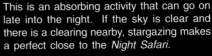

Pit Viper

Age Level: any age (6 and up)
Skills/Subject Areas: science, relationships in Nature, listening skills, problem solving,
Eco-Concepts:
 Interdependence - all things are connected to and depend on other living things
 Adaptation - everything has evolved to fit how and where it lives
Required Materials: blindfolds, an object to mark the 'mouse hole'
Prep Time: none
Classroom Adaptations/Variations: research and discuss local snakes and their importance in the environment and which species control rodent pests

Description:

Pit Viper is a game that emphasizes predator/prey interactions in an interactive, experiential way.

The pit viper is a large, sedentary predator that seizes small mammals as they come within close range of its hiding place. Jungle rats are one of the snake's favorite foods. Vipers employ heat sensors located in deep 'pits' behind the nose as well as huge, night-vision eyes to locate their prey.

In the game, most players become 'jungle rats' leaving their burrows at sundown and scrambling off in search of seeds, fruit, and insects. A few players become 'pit vipers' and are positioned by an instructor between the 'rat's' home 'burrow' and the scattered jungle rat players. The pit viper players must lie down and cannot move from the spot where they were placed except to reach out and grab any 'jungle rats' that approach close enough to be 'eaten'.

To replicate the advantage the pit vipers have with their superb camouflage and surprise-ambush style of predation, all jungle rat players are blindfolded throughout the exercise. When the instructor announces that morning is coming and all 'jungle rats' must now return to their 'burrows', the real action begins.

'Jungle rats', of course, must be very quiet as they work their way back to their home burrows, blindfolded. If they should bump into one another, they can touch each other with their arms and hands, but no sounds must be uttered. A 'jungle rat' seized by a 'pit viper' can send out an alarm squeal to warn others of the danger. If the 'pit viper' does not get a good hold on the jungle rat player's arm or leg, and the 'rat' is able to break free and escape, then it is still 'alive' but without the use of the affected limb for the remainder of the game. 'Jungle rats' lucky enough to make it back safely to their 'burrow' (either wounded or fully intact) can remove their blindfolds and be silent spectators to the remaining action. This game can be played most anywhere, as long as a common point of touch origin is established beforehand as the place from

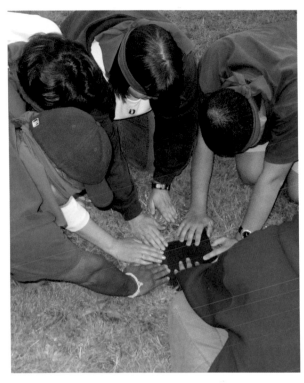

which all 'jungle rats' originate and to which they want to return. A large rock or mound of earth or the base of a tree works well. This activity can easily be adapted to different bio-regions.

Try alternating the pit viper/jungle rat players with praying mantis/fly, wolfeel/fish, or sea anemone/minnow, to help participants learn about different ecosystems and similar sedentary predator/moving-prey interactions.

Population Pond

Age Level: any age (6 and up)
Skills/Subject Areas: math, science, knowledge of flora and fauna, observation, cooperative learning, problem solving
Required Materials: large fresh water basin and duck weed *(Lemna minor)*
Prep Time: medium - 15-20 minutes
Classroom Adaptations/Variations: graph a 'J' curve and discuss exponential growth in relationship to human population

Description:

Of all the dilemmas humanity will face in this millennium there may be none more challenging than population growth. "Whatever your cause, it's a lost cause without population stabilization," reads a popular t-shirt slogan worn by some concerned citizens.

Of course, people have been debating the Earth's carrying capacity for ages, certainly since the time of Socrates, if not before. Dire predictions of overpopulation leading to global famine, pandemic diseases and complete social breakdown have been put forward for centuries. To date, none have come to full fruition in threatening the survival of our species.

So far advances in food production and medicine have been able to keep pace with our growing numbers; but how long can science save us from our reproductive success? We all know that in a world of finite resources, no species can keep growing exponentially in numbers without serious ultimate consequences.

It is hard to fathom the speed with which humanity is now populating the Earth. Consider for example that during our past 100,000 years of human existence as hunter/gatherer societies, the world's population was increasing one person every five years. Today we are expanding at a rate of nearly three people every second.

It was the advent of agriculture during the past 8 to 10 thousand years that brought about the ability to expand our numbers exponentially. We have seen a doubling of the human population in the last 50 years alone, from three to six billion. Our numbers are expected to nearly double again by the later half of this century before it shows signs of leveling off at eleven to twelve billion.

But can we fully grasp this phenomenal rate of growth? Children grow up learning to count on their fingers. Only at advanced stages in their brain development can they master more complex mathematical thought patterns. Experiential growth is a mathematical concept that can confound even adults.

Population Pond is a simple exercise that helps students understand in the most graphically visual way what is happening with the world's population. The exercise takes 100 days to complete, but requires no effort on the part of the participants other than simple daily observation.

You will need a one meter wide basin of water for this exercise. A plastic basin set in one corner of your classroom (near a window or under sufficient artificial light) will suffice, but it is much nicer to use an outdoor setting. A small cement pond, or water crock with a few guppies swimming in it, set in the school yard, will hold more interest for students.

The focal point of a *Population Pond* is a single strand of 'duck weed' *(Lemna minor)*, a freshwater aquatic plant that floats freely on the surface of ponds. This tiny plant with 2-3 bright green leaves and a short root system that suspends from the leaves, has the prolific ability to reproduce itself (vegetatively) every 24 hours. If, for instance, you have one plant on day one, you will have two on day 2, four on day 3, eight on day 4, sixteen on day 5, and so on. This is exponential growth.

Duck weed can be found on the surface of many quiet ponds throughout the world and it is sold as an ornamental aquatic plant at many nurseries. You only need a single strand for this exercise, so there should be no cost in acquiring one.

Have a little ceremony with your class on the day you set your strand of duckweed on the water of your *Population Pond*. Tell your students that this single plant symbolizes our human ancestors back in the days when we were all hunter/gatherers, and that the next 100 days will represent all human time since the advent of agriculture. If your pond is the right size and conditions are optimum for growth, in 100 days time it should be completely covered in duck weed.

See how many students can correctly predict the day on which the pond will be half covered. Many will say the 50th day, so be sure to have the entire class inspect the pond on that day. It won't have much coverage at all. The correct answer, of course, is the 99th day. Be sure to have everyone pay close attention on that day as well as the following day when the surface area of vegetation will suddenly double and no water surface will show.

Place a male and female guppy (Poecilia reticulata) in your pond to prevent any mosquito larvae from developing. If they are adequately fed, your students may be amazed at how many offspring they have sired in the same 100 days in which the duck weed was reproducing.

There should be more to the *Population Pond* exercise than the comprehension of a mathematical principle. If humanity is now approaching that "99th day" whereby the total population (that took 2 million years to reach 6 billion) suddenly doubles in a few decades, then we'd better start preparing for it.

What can we do? Get used to crowds for starters. Human tolerance and compassion for one another will be put to its greatest test. Conservation of natural resources will be another critical factor in sustaining a massive population, stabilizing it, and eventually getting it more in sync with a sustainable population. Water conservation will be crucial (see: *Water Wasters / Water Savers pgs.96-99*), as will food production, distribution, and eating lower on the food chain. Most importantly, humanity will have to come back to the realization that Nature's laws still apply to us, we cannot pretend to separate ourselves from them (see: *Simple Bear Necessities pgs.90-91*).

Rabbit Run

Age Level: any age (6 and up)
Skills/Subject Areas: P.E., science, energy burner, relationships in Nature
Eco-Concepts:
    Interdependence - all things are connected to and depend on other living things
    Adaptation - everything has evolved to fit how and where it lives
Required Materials: headbands to distinguish 'coyotes', survey tape or scarves for 'rabbit holes', scrub brush, carrot and celery sticks, prize for winning team (optional)
Prep Time: low- less than 10 minutes

Description:

"Have you ever noticed how a rabbit uses speed, camouflage, and safe burrows to avoid equally fast predators like fox, lynx, coyote, and wolf?" a leader asks the group. "Well, lets see how it feels to be both the pursuer and the pursued; let's do a *Rabbit Run!*"

Choose a large playing field for this exercise and mark off two end zones at least fifty meters apart. Now mark out six to eight small circles (approximately one meter in diameter) throughout the field of play. Brightly colored survey tape or colored kerchiefs work well for this purpose. These are the 'rabbit burrows' or 'holes'; any time a fleeing 'rabbit' jumps into one of these 'holes', he or she is safe.

Next, scatter throughout the field six to eight branches pruned from trees or scrub brush. This serves the 'rabbits' as camouflage. Any time a rabbit player freezes holding a piece of this brush, the 'rabbit' is completely camouflaged and the predators can't see it.

Finally, position two staff members at opposite ends holding celery sticks as rewards for successful 'rabbits'.

Now that the field is set up,

divide the group and explain the rules. One-quarter of the players will become predators – 'fox, lynx, coyote, or wolf'. The remaining seventy-five percent will be the 'rabbits'. Divide the rabbit players into two groups and position them to start at opposite ends of the field. The object of the game for the 'rabbits' is to cross the field as many times as possible, collecting one celery stick or one carrot stick each time they reach an end zone. They can avoid predators by hopping into a 'hole' or by camouflaging in a freeze position holding the brush. However, only one rabbit player at a time can occupy a 'hole' or camouflage position, and they must vacate the protected position as soon as another 'rabbit' approaches their place of refuge.

Any 'rabbit' on the run that is caught by a predator must forfeit one of their celery or carrot sticks to that predator and return to the nearest end zone to start their run over. Predators are free to develop hunting strategies as a group but they can only tag moving 'rabbits', and only the 'coyote' that tags one is entitled to one of their carrot or celery sticks.

When all the celery and carrot sticks are gone from staff members in the end zone, the game is over. At this point call everyone together to count the number of sticks they have. Acknowledge or award a prize to the 'rabbit' that holds the most celery and carrot sticks, and the 'coyote' that captured the most.

This is a very lively and fast-paced predator/prey interactive game that can burn off some of that extra energy just before mealtime. The bottom line in this activity is that the kids will have eaten their vegetables before dinner.

89

Simple Bear Necessities

Age Level: any age (6 and up)
Skills/Subject Areas: math, science, data collection, cooperative learning, energy burner, relationships in Nature
Eco-Concepts:
   Cycles - Nature works in cycles; the building materials for life must be used over and over again
   Change - everything is in the process of becoming something else
   Interdependence - all things are connected to and depend on other living things
Required Materials: poster board graph, felt pen, cut outs of fish, trees and rain drops
Prep Time: high - 30 minutes or more
Classroom Adaptations/Variations: research examples of population dynamics that demonstrates how overpopulation taxes available resources

Description:

This is a fast paced exercise that combines fun with learning important lessons about population dynamics and human impacts on wildlife.

"What are the simple bear necessities - the things, besides air, that all animals require?" the facilitator asks a group of students that have gathered in an open field, or large play area. "Food, water, and shelter," should be the answer the students have no trouble coming up with. "Ok, good," the instructor continues, "we're going to play a game where half of you will become 'bears' and the other half will represent 'habitat' – the simple bear necessities of food, water or shelter."

It is important to explain the different roles of 'bear' and 'habitat' to the entire group as they will be constantly interchanging their positions. Both teams start out 20-30 meters apart at opposite ends of a play field. With their backs to the opposing team, the 'bear' players choose one of three positions to indicate their need: 'food', 'water' or 'shelter'. They hold both hands over their stomach to indicate the need for food, both hands over the mouth to indicate the need for water, and they form a canopy above their head with outstretched arms if they require shelter. The bear players choose these positions individually, so that during any given period of play, all three habitat positions should be in use.

The habitat players, with their backs turned to the 'bears' and standing at the opposite end of the field, can use the same hand and arm positions to decide what they choose to be during each round of play. It is much more visual, however, to use cut out cards in the shape of fish, water drops and trees to designate food, water and shelter. The only other prop required for this exercise is a poster board with a simple graph drawn on it that shows number of bears over time. If you have 20 players make certain that the vertical line on your graph goes up from zero x 20. The horizontal time line can be shown in ten year increments up to 100 years.

The activity begins with the instructor telling both teams to choose a position, and then on the count of three to turn and face one another. Bear players must hold the positions with their hands as they run across the field to match up with a habitat player that holds a card (or the same hand position) and thereby meets their need. Only the first 'bear' that holds the hand position for water, for instance, and runs to a water droplet is successful; other bear players having the same need must find a different person. A 'bear' that successfully meets its need reproduces by taking their habitat player with them as a new 'bear cub'. Those 'bears' that are unsuccessful in meeting their needs, die and become habitat players. It is impor-

On the 10th round of play, the habitat players can be instructed to turn around holding very few or no cards at all. The bears will stop running half way across the field. "That's totally unfair," some bear player is likely to complain. "You can't take away our water too." "Sure we can," the instructor replies, "We've decided to divert the rivers you depend on to water our crops and the golf courses we've planted in the desert."

tant to remind habitat players to set down their habitat cards before they cross the field. To avoid confusion, it is also important to remind them to only hold one card when they turn to face the bears; the remaining two cards can be set on the ground or held behind their backs.

The instructor (or a student assigned the task), carefully counts the number of 'bears' after each round of play and graphs the number on the chart. Ten rounds of play should show a cyclical rise and fall in bear numbers over time. To dramatize the exercise, the instructor can ask all of the habitat players in round number 8 to set down their tree cards before turning and facing the bear players. "That's not fair," a bear player in need of shelter is likely to complain when they can't find a person holding a tree card. "That's right, it isn't fair," the teacher can answer. "Perhaps that's how bears feel when so much of their former range is deforested, turned into farmland, or expanding suburban developments."

Try playing round number 9 by having the habitat players not use their food (fish) cards. Cries of foul play are sure to arise again from hungry bear players that had to die from lack of fish. "Sorry," the instructor might apologize, "we forgot about you bears when we set our human quotas for the fish catch this year."

If you play out these last three scenarios, your graph will show a dramatic decline in bear numbers in the last few decades. Bring everyone together to sit in a circle to discuss this.

All animal populations show periodic rises and declines in their numbers that are cyclical over time. Rabbits, for instance, show shorter cycles than bears. But the chart clearly illustrates what happens to animals that lose too many of their basic necessities. Ask the students to determine at what point in their 100-year graph did the 'bears' become endangered? Did their activity actually result in extinction? What about humans? Are we as a species immune from Nature's laws?

Over top of the bear population graph use a different colored felt pen to show the human population fifty years ago; then double that for the present population. Projecting another doubling of human numbers within the first half of this century, the students should be looking at a graph of exponential growth. "Can human numbers keep increasing at this rate indefinitely?" the instructor might ask. "At what point do you think our population might level off and start to decline? Do you think there's any correlation between rapidly expanding human numbers and rapidly declining wildlife populations?"

Storm

Description:

Oceans cover 71% of the Earth's surface and contain 96.5% of its water. We should really be referring to our home as planet 'Water', not planet Earth. If you smoothed out our planet's crust - filling the ocean floor with the dry land of the continents - the Earth's entire surface would be covered by nearly 3,000 meters of sea water. Too bad sea water is virtually unusable for humans.

"So where does our freshwater come from?" students might well ask. The answer lies in one of the greatest forces on Earth - the hydrologic (water) cycle. Heat from the sun evaporates water from the surface of the Earth, converting it from a liquid to gaseous state. This salt-free water vapor then rises to form clouds that gradually condense into massive storm clouds releasing fresh water in the form of rain back to the surface.

Though clouds and water vapor hold a mere .004% of all fresh water, they still contain six times more water than all the world's rivers. Students curious as to where the rest of the fresh water on Earth is to be found might be interested in the fact that nearly 70% of it is frozen in polar ice caps, glaciers, permanent snow and permafrost. Another 30% of all fresh water is underground, most of it in deep, hard to reach aquifers. Lakes and rivers combined contain just a little more than one-fourth of one percent of all fresh water - something to think about when we carelessly contaminate these small reserves.

Evaporation is only part of the story of how water from the surface of the Earth becomes vaporized into clouds; transpiration plays another important role. Trees absorb ground water through their roots and transfer it to nourish their leaves. They do this by drawing water up through their phloem, the living tissue under the bark. During daylight hours the sun gets so strong that it draws some of the water through the pores of the leaves, vaporizes it, and it too contributes to forming clouds.

Storm is a fun, experiential activity developed by youth attending a Rediscovery International Leadership Training at Canada's United World College. It helps students understand the role of evaporation and transpiration in the hydrologic cycle. A few props are necessary for this exercise. A large (queen or king size) bed sheet can be used for the 'cloud'. A yellow head scarf, worn by one player, can suffice for the 'sun', though a cut out from cardboard or dense foam with yellow ribbons attached for rays, is much more dramatic. The bulk of the players in this exercise become either 'water' or 'trees'. Here again, blue and green head bands can be used, but construction board or plastic

sheet cut-outs in the shape of rain drops and tree outlines makes the exercise more visual.

Storm is an all out action exercise and energy burner, but it becomes much more educational through a good introduction and closing session. "What powers the water cycle on Earth; what is the driving force that can vaporize water into clouds?" the instructor might ask. The first student that correctly answers, "The sun!" has the privilege of playing that role or passing it on to another player that is a fast runner.

The instructor then needs to remind the students of the ways in which water is converted to water vapor and clouds through evaporation and transpiration. Diagrams work well here as a teaching aid. Approximately half of the students are selected to play the role of 'water' by wearing blue head bands, or holding cut outs of a water droplet. The remaining students become 'trees' with green head bands or by holding cut outs of evergreen or deciduous trees. The instructor can choose a few students to help them hold the four corners of the sheet that becomes the 'cloud'.

Before the activity begins, the students must clearly understand all of the roles as they become interchangeable to some extent during the exercise. Tree players all start out spread throughout the play area crouched low to the ground, like a seed waiting to sprout. When a water player touches them gently with their raindrop cut-out, they grow into a half squat position. They hold this stance until another water player touches them again. With each 'raindrop' touch a tree player grows taller from crouch to half squat, to fully standing, to raising one arm (like a branch), to raising the second arm. When the 'tree' is fully grown it is transpiring so much water that it will actually trade places with the next water player that comes by to nourish it.

Throughout the game, the sun player is chasing the water players, and gently tagging them with the cut-out sun symbol. Each water player that gets tagged immediately vaporizes with a loud hiss and goes under the 'cloud'. The cloud players are constantly drifting slowly throughout the play area until they get 4-5 players under their sheet. They then stop and flap the sheet wildly shouting, "Storm!" as all the raindrops release to go out and nourish more 'trees'. Good cloud players should make for very "bad hair days" for the water players with their sheet flapping.

Another element to add to the exercise is the effect of acid rain on the forest. Black 'raindrops' with skull and cross bones painted on (or just black head bands) can be used to distinguish acid rain players. After a few rounds of general play, some of the water players that come under the 'cloud' can have their 'raindrops' or blue head bands exchanged for black ones. When they are released from the 'cloud' following a 'storm,' they continue to touch tree players, but each time they do so the 'tree' dies back one position. The blue water players can always help the 'tree' back to its former healthy state, but as more and more acid rain players are added to the game, it becomes very difficult for the tree players to stay upright.

Discuss the impacts of acid rain on forests once the game concludes - usually when everyone is quite winded. "When does the water cycle end?" the instructor might ask the group. "Never," should be the obvious answer. "At least not until the sun in our solar system burns out," the instructor might add. "What about at night, when there is no sunlight?" the instructor might challenge the students. "Is there still evaporation and transpiration in the dark?" Because over half of the Earth is always in sunlight, and even a dry wind can cause evaporation at night, only transpiration from trees slows down during night hours.

Storm is a simple exercise, but a dramatic one in helping youngsters understand a cycle in Nature that affects us all profoundly every day. While it may seem geared for elementary students, it has been tried and tested equally successful with all age groups, including professional adults.

Snail Trail

Age Level: any age (6 and up)
Skills/Subject Areas: awareness, tuning in to Nature, observation skills
Required Materials: toothpicks, trail
Prep Time: medium- 15-20 minutes

Description:

Snail Trail is a simple yet powerful introductory lesson to any outdoor activity or environmental topic.

The instructor will need to scout out a trail and place toothpicks randomly in and adjacent to the trail before they take the participants hiking. The instructor can place these in trees, plants or wherever they desire, but at least half of the toothpick must be visible and above ground. Remember to keep track of how many toothpicks are hidden along the trail. It will help later when the students look for them. It also helps to keep the toothpicks within a few meters of the middle of the trail.

The instructor then guides the participants down the trail containing the toothpicks, deliberately racing past the toothpicks and distracting the participants from noticing

them. After the instructor gives an introduction about awareness and tuning their senses in to their surroundings, she/he then announces, "We've just walked past a lot of interesting things on the trail. Take some time. Go back a few hundred meters on the trail but this time, engage your senses. Slow down, be as slow as a snail if necessary; take time to notice things you might have missed."

As the students slow down and retrace their route they will begin to discover how many interesting things they were oblivious to as they hiked rapidly and distracted through the forest. Hopefully they will also see all of the toothpicks that are on and near the trail. Challenge the students to find as many as they can.

After the activity a discussion is easily facilitated about the fact that we go through life hardly in tune with our surroundings. We speed along, constantly trying to reach destinations at the expense of enjoying the journey. This is especially true in the modern, busy lives we lead. In order to begin to enjoy the outdoors or appreciate Nature, people of all ages must slow down, take the time to notice things and appreciate the world they are a part of and immersed in.

Water Wasters/Water Savers

Age Level: any age (6 and up)
Skills/Subject Areas: science, energy burner, cooperative learning,
Eco-Concept:
   Cycles - Nature works in cycles; the building materials for life must be used over and over again
Required Materials: one large bucket, two small buckets, small plastic or paper cups, head bands or arm bands to distinguish 'water wasters' from 'water savers'
Prep Time: low - less than 10 minutes
Classroom Adaptations/Variations: determine water use in the school and at home, discuss conservation of water

Description:

For a world that is more than 70% water, things are drying up awfully fast. Only 2.5% of the planet's water is fresh and a mere fraction of that is available for human use. It is said that there will be wars fought in this century, not for land, but for water. "Unless we take swift and decisive action," UN Secretary General Koffi Anan has warned, "by 2025, two-thirds of the world's population will be living in countries that face serious water shortages."

It all sounds pretty scary, and it can be a depressing topic for young people who have their whole lives ahead of them, but it is not hopeless. The answer is to get smart about how we use water. There are many things we can do in our daily lives, at home, school, and the work place, that allow us to be part of the solution rather than contribute to the problem.

Water conservation is the obvious place to start. Consider the fact that every person on the planet (currently 6.5 billion, but projected to be 11 billion by the later half of this century) requires 50 liters of water per day for drinking, bathing, cooking and other basic needs. Now consider the amount of water we waste in our daily lives; just a few toilet flushes requires 50 liters.

Water Wasters/ Water Savers is a simple and fun exercise designed to engage participants and lead them into frank discussions on making behavioral changes in their lives. You will need three plastic buckets for this exercise and small plastic drinking cups for two-thirds of the players. Set out one big bucket in the middle of a grassy playing field and the other two buckets 20-30 meters away from the center on opposite ends of the field. The number of players you have will determine the distance. If you have 30-40 participants, make the distance larger so that there is plenty of open space for everyone to run about.

The two buckets on opposite ends of the field start out completely empty, but the center bucket is filled with water (12.5 liters for a small group / 25 liters for a large group). These volumes correspond with one or two flushes of a standard toilet.

Now call all of your players into a circle and have them count themselves out 1 to 3. Everyone that called out numbers 1 and 3 are given blue head bands and sent off in different teams to the empty water buckets on opposite ends of the field. They are to be the

'Water Savers'. The players that remain (number 2's) are given black headbands and sent to the center of the field near the full water bucket. They are to be the 'Water Wasters'. The Water Waster team must quickly think of ways that water is wasted every day. Examples: 1) not turning off the shower faucet while lathering with soap, 2) washing clothes without a full load, 3) leaving the tap water running while brushing teeth, 4) running the dishwasher with just a few items to clean, 5) leaving the hose running while washing the car, 6) watering the lawn in the noon day sun, 7) not turning off (or fixing) a leaky tap, etc.

The object of the game is for 'Water Savers' to fill their respective buckets as quickly as possible by drawing one cup of water at a time from the central bucket. All the while, 'Water Wasters' are trying to tag and challenge the 'Water Savers' by asking a question they must honestly answer. For instance: "Do you always turn off the tap when you are brushing your teeth?" If the answer is, "Yes, I always do," then that Water Saver player is allowed to run off with their cup of water. If the answer is, "No", "Not always", or a sheepish "Sometimes," then the 'Water Waster player gets to douse the Water Saver player with their cup of water.

To slow down, and make things more difficult for the 'Water Wasters', a Water Saver player can tag them each time they return to the central well with their empty cup. Once tagged, a 'Water Waster' must stop and turn on the spot 3 times before they can pursue other 'Water Savers' hauling water.

The exercise gets pretty wild as you can well imagine with water dousing involved. It is best to do this activity on a hot sunny day so everyone dries off quickly and the grass gets a bit of watering. If it is a cool overcast

day, or the facilitator needs to keep their charges dry, they can simply instruct the 'Water Wasters' to dump out the cup of water on the ground instead of dousing the opposing player.

The game is not over until the central water bucket is completely empty. Call together the two teams of 'Water Savers' with their buckets to the center to see which has managed to save the most water. Acknowledge the more successful of the two teams and give them the reward of determining the best use of the water they saved. That use can range from watering plants in the schoolyard to giving all the players an unexpected bath by tossing the water high into the air.

Now that you have gotten everyone's attention and burned some excess energy, sit down with your students and challenge them to compile a list of ways they can conserve water in their daily lives. More important than making the list, of course, is implementing it. After all, they've all just squandered a fair bit of water; it's time to make some amends.

Pick one water conservation strategy at a time to be implemented, and challenge everyone in your class to focus on that goal for an entire week. Make a poster to hang in your classroom to remind them: "It's Turn Off the Shower While Soaping Up Week!" Divide the class into two teams and get a show of hands each day to see how many did and did not meet this objective. Keep score. By the end of the week you should be getting 100% compliance from both teams through peer pressure alone. Now choose a second water conservation strategy for

week number two, while the week one action continues and becomes habit forming.

By the end of 14 weeks, you should be able to implement all of the water conservation strategies listed below. If you don't think your class actions are making a difference in the world, try calculating the water your group has conserved in that 3.5 month period. It's staggering.

14 WATER CONSERVATION TIPS FOR DAILY LIFE

1) Flush only when necessary. Avoid using a toilet as a waste basket; each flush uses between 12.5-25 liters of water.
2) Only use your dishwasher when you have a full load, and set it to the cycle with the least number of washes and rinses.
3) Avoid running water continuously when washing dishes in a sink. Use separate sides of the sink for washing and rinsing.
4) Wash your dishes only once a day.
5) Do not clean fruits and vegetables under running tap water. Use a basin and then water your house plants with the same water.
6) Avoid running the tap to get cold drinking water, keep a bottle of drinking water in your refrigerator instead.
7) Decide before you bathe - shower or tub? Only a very short shower saves more water than a partially filled tub. A full bathtub, however, uses 164-273 liters of water - more than a short shower.
8) Do not let the water run in the sink while shaving, brushing teeth, or lathering your face and hands.
9) Wash clothes only with a full load and avoid permanent press cycles they use an extra 55-110 liters of water.
10) Compost or dispose of food waste instead of grinding it down the garbage disposal. Disposals not only use a great deal of water, they can clog your septic field with grease.

11) Water your lawn and garden and wash your car only when absolutely necessary.
12) Water your lawn before 10 a.m., or in the evening, to avoid rapid evaporation.
13) Use a broom instead of a hose when cleaning walkways and driveways.
14) Wash your car with a bucket and rinse it with a hose that has a shut off nozzle.

MORE WATER CONSERVATION IDEAS

- Eliminate leaks in faucets, toilets, hoses and pipes. The leak from a 1/32" opening in a faucet or pipe can waste up to 32.760 liters of water per month. A steady drip from a tap wastes 110 liters per day.

- Install low-flow aerators on all faucets. The water flow will seem stronger, but you will actually reduce consumption by 50%.

- Check toilets for leaks by adding food coloring to the toilet tank. If color appears in the bowl (without flushing), you have a leak that could be wasting over 1,000 liters of water a day without making a sound.

- Buy a 'suds-saver' washing machine when you replace an old one for greatly reduced water consumption.

- Use water-efficient sprinklers and timing devices to aid absorption by the soil. Water overflowing onto the side walk and gutter is a great waste.

- A drip irrigation system in your garden waters the root areas of your plants and can save up to 60% over other watering techniques.

- Turn off your water and hot water heater when going on a long trip.

Web of Life

Age Level: any age (6 and up)
Skills/Subject Areas: science, knowledge of local flora and fauna, cooperative learning
Eco-Concept:
   Interdependence - all things are connected to and depend on other living things
Required Materials: species cards, large ball of rope/string, index cards, pens and ink pad
Prep Time: high - 30 minutes or more

Description:

"Whenever we try to single out anything by itself in Nature, we find it hitched to everything else in the universe." So wrote Ralph Waldo Emerson more than a century ago. Yet, even in this age of environmental awareness, it is still difficult to grasp the incredible complexity and interrelatedness of all living things. *Web of Life* is a simple exercise, but one that helps youngsters better understand life's connections.

You will need a long spool of string for this activity. Kite string wound onto a spool with handles works very well because it can be quickly dispensed and is easy to rewind for future use. You will also need index cards with the names of species found in your bio-region printed on the face of each card. Photographs of animals and plants, cut from magazines and mounted on index cards or poster board, can be even more effective in portraying this exercise, but will, of course, require considerably more effort.

In a comfortable location, have everyone sit close together in a circle and distribute one card to each player. If you have fewer than twenty players, give out two cards per player (one for each hand). *Web of Life* requires at least a dozen players to ensure sufficient species for the interconnections; twenty to forty players would be ideal.

Have fun while distributing the cards: "You're a mule deer, you're a fungus, you're a grizzly bear, you're a maggot," the instructor says to the players while handing out the cards. Ask everyone to set their cards out in front of them, i.e., one in front of a foot or propped up against the knees, so that hands are free and all others in the circle can read everyone else's species titles.

Examples of species in a Pacific Northwest forest ecosystem might include:

1.	Bald Eagle	31.	Deer
2.	Red-tailed Hawk	32.	Squirrel
3.	Peregrine Falcon	33.	Bat
4.	Mallard	34.	Shrew
5.	Canada Goose	35.	Mice
6.	Great Horned Owl	36.	Frog
7.	Kingfisher	37.	Salamander
8.	Crow	38.	Salmon
9.	Raven	39.	Trout
10.	Swallow	40.	Stickleback (fish)
11.	Woodpecker	41.	Dragonfly
12	Thrush	42.	Mayfly
13.	Hummingbird	43.	Mosquito
14.	Wren	44.	Moths
15.	Great Blue Heron	45.	Ants
16.	Black Bear	46.	Black Flies
17.	Cougar	47.	Wood Ticks
18.	Wolf	48.	Maggots
19.	Coyote	49.	No-See-Ums
20.	Grizzly Bear	50.	Slugs
21.	Fox	51.	Earthworms
22.	Marten	52.	Bacteria
23.	Raccoon	53.	Termites
24.	Land Otter	54.	Lichen
25.	Weasel	55.	Mushrooms
26.	Beaver	56.	Blueberry
27.	Rabbit	57.	Hemlock
28.	Porcupine	58.	Aspen
29.	Lynx	59.	Huckleberry
30.	Moose	60.	Spruce Tree

These, of course, are just a few of the many thousands of species found in this bio-region, so the *Web of Life* is always grossly oversimplified.

The exercise can begin anywhere. "Who wants to start?" the leader asks. "I do," shouts a frog card-holder. "Okay, you hold the end of the string," the leader continues. "What is something a frog eats, or eats a frog?" "Frogs eat mosquitoes," someone offers. "That's exactly right," the leader says, unwinding the string from the 'frog' to the person holding the mosquito card. "Now what else eats a mosquito or what does a mosquito eat?" the instructor continues.

Possibilities here are many: trout, salmon, stickleback fish, salamander, dragonfly, swallow, wren, bats, and bacteria all eat mosquitoes. Mosquitoes in turn will feed on only warm-blooded creatures, which means any mammal or bird in the circle of players.

The string continues to connect the circle. Anytime the group gets stuck, they can al-

ways go back to 'bacteria', which breaks down everything dead. It is important for the leader of this exercise to have a good grounding in biology, or just bush knowledge and common sense. Most of the connections the participants will be able to make themselves, without much prompting. When they get stuck the leader should help them out.

Very quickly, the *Web of Life* starts to resemble a very intricately connected spider web. When it reaches the point that it's very difficult for the leader to step through the spaces to make connections, or the string runs out, it is time for some further lessons.

"Consider this," the leader says, "if we were able to establish every possible connection here, this web of string would be so thick that we wouldn't be able to see through it. Remember, we are representing only a fraction of the species found in this area and we are illustrating the most basic food-web relationships. Species influence and depend on one another not just for food, but in many more complex ways."

"Now let's look at what happens if some species in this circle are threatened," the instructor continues. "What happens when DDT enters the food chain of eagles and their eggs become so thin eagles cannot reproduce?" The player holding the string with all the eagle connections is asked to lightly tug on it so everyone feels the connection. There are many scenarios that can be explored - effects of deforestation (tree species and all animals dependant upon them tug their strings), wolf-control programs, over fishing, water diversion and wetland reclamation - sadly the list of impact scenarios is all too real.

Now the instructor walks around the outer perimeter of the circle of participants assigning a number (1 to 4) to each person, or a number to each person's hand if players are all holding two species cards.

If the *Web of Life* has been created with climbing rope, a small person can be laid out on their back with arms outstretched across the strands of the web.

"Let's see if this web of life is strong and intricate enough to support humans," the facilitator says as he/she instructs everyone in the circle to stand up holding their rope tight. There is a great feeling of support at this point and everyone can see that humanity is part of the web.

"But, wait a minute," the facilitator continues, "scientists say that Earth could experience a 25% biodiversity loss in our lifetime. Let's see what that looks like."

"Pick a number from one to four," the facilitator instructs the person lying in the middle of the 'web'. "Three!" he or she answers. "All the '3s', let go of your string when I count to three," says the facilitator.

The great *Web of Life* goes limp and the person in the middle now finds themselves on the floor (proof that humanity is not just part of the web, but also greatly dependent on its interrelatedness).

"This is what is predicted to happen on Earth in the not too distant future if we don't act now to help save our planet's treasure trove of life," the facilitator continues as she or he passes out index cards and pens to everyone standing in the circle. "The important thing here is that this has not fully happened yet, and it must not happen. We must all commit to taking individual action in our own lives to ensure a 25% biodiversity loss never happens."

Everyone is encouraged to find a private meditative place in Nature where they make a promise to themselves to do one or more significant things in their lives to ensure that this scenario never comes about. An ink pad is set out for each person to seal their promise with a fingerprint.

"No one knows for certain, but it is believed that your fingerprint is unique. No one else shares the unique pattern of your fingerprint," the facilitator concludes. "You are extraordinarily distinct, as is every creature on Earth - creatures we depend upon to continue our own lineage."

When the group comes back together some may wish to share with others the personal commitment they made.

103

their watershed. Traditional Maori in New Zealand, for example, have a strong sense of place. They are known to state the name of their mountain, their river and their sea before giving their own name at a formal function.

Challenge your students to do the same. On a sheet of paper see how many of them can draw a map of their watershed that places their home and school correctly within it. Ask them to name the highest point of land from which their watershed flows. Ask them to name the main river that drains their watershed to the sea and show the course of major tributaries. Finally, challenge them to name the bay, sound, inlet or open sea that their river flows in to.

Chances are your students will perform this assignment rather dismally, which is all the more reason to engage them more fully in it. Help them go back to the source from which all waters flow - rain fall or snow and ice melt - and let your students discover for themselves how a watershed works.

On a very rainy day, surprise your class. "Wow, it's such a beautiful day today; I think we should all go for a walk outdoors."

Don rain gear, or grab umbrellas, and head out for a little watershed walk-about. Have each student pretend they are a single raindrop that has fallen on the spot where they are standing in the school yard. Where would that raindrop go? Would it absorb into the ground, or start running over the surface of a paved area?

Look for rain accumulating in puddles on the school steps, sidewalks, courtyard, parking lot or roadway. Are there small puddles overflowing into larger puddles at slightly lower elevations? Follow the flow downhill. You are now moving with the influence of gravity along the course of your watershed. Keep following it. Does it flow into a ditch or stream, a pond or lake? If so where does the stream flow to, where does the lake exit? Follow it.

Where's My Watershed?

Age Level: any age (6 and up)
Skills/Subject Areas: science, data collection, observation, cooperative learning, technology, team building, citizenship, speaking skills, problem solving, relationships in Nature
Eco-Concepts:
  Cycles - Nature works in cycles; the building materials for life must be used over and over again
  Change - everything is in the process of becoming something else
  Community - animals and plants live together in special areas that meet their need
Required Materials: topographical maps of your area, pen, paper,
Prep Time: high - 30 minutes or more

Description:

We all live within a watershed, though most urban dwellers seem little aware of it. A watershed is the entire area of land drained by a river system, from the highest point of land to the point where the river enters the sea.

Indigenous peoples worldwide often have a profound knowledge of, and relationship to,

Does your water course flow to a metal grate along the curb and go down a storm drain? If so it's not game over, just time to adjust your research a bit. You will now need to visit your municipality's water board, or search their web site for the city's storm drainage plans. Make that task a homework assignment for part of your class while the others try to get the same information from parents and neighbors. The students may be surprised to learn that most adults are as clueless as they are about where water flows when it disappears underground.

By the next class session, the students' research should have given them a much better picture of the water drainage patterns in their neighborhood. Now it's time to pull out the topographical maps to get the big picture.

Here again, few students will have the skills necessary to read contour lines on a topographical map. You can help them by means of a simple exercise. Instruct each student sitting at their station to make a fist with one hand and place it (folded fingers down) atop the desk. Have them peer at their hand from a side angle, pretending it is a mountain. Now tell them to identify the highest point (usually the bone protruding from the base of the middle finger) and draw a small circle around that 'summit' with a pen. Next, instruct them to draw another circle slightly below the first. If they look carefully they will discover that the bone at the base of the index finger is at this same height as their second contour line; draw a circle around that height as well.

Continue drawing the contours of the hand all the way down to where it touches the desk (photo pg.106). When everyone has completed their contours instruct them to lay their hands flat atop the desk. Suddenly, your students will understand the concept of a topographical map - vertical contours displayed in a horizontal plane. Test their comprehension of this principle by having them identify the highest and lowest points on a real topographical map.

Now everyone has the skills they will need to draw out their entire watershed on a detailed topographical map. You will need larger scale maps for this if, for instance, your school is in a major watershed like the Mississippi, Yukon, Amazon, Nile or the Danube rivers. Even if your watershed starts at a continental divide, challenge your students to trace the outline on a map from the highest point of land to where it enters the sea. Once they have established the boundaries, set out to explore it.

once lived within it; do they still? How did they live in the past, today? To what extent were the rivers in your watershed arteries for travel throughout history? How have settlement patterns changed over time? Has the watershed been altered - damed or diverted - in any way? How would you assess the overall health of your watershed? Are there still healthy fish populations, or has your waterway become an open sewer, a dumping ground for hazardous wastes from industry, homes and schools?

All of these questions and more can stimulate student discussions and integrate knowledge from the core subjects (science, social studies, reading, writing, math, health and the arts). A single environmental education project like this can help students meet many learning requirements at one time.

A watershed walk-about is almost never completed in a single class session or outing. It is rather a series of discoveries over time, all of which contribute to an expanding and profound sense of place. It might take years for a school group to explore a very large watershed, but a lot of this exploration can be combined with school field trips, or even family vacations. Students doing extra-curricular work like this can report back to their class later through written assignments or power-point presentations. They should be acknowledged and receive course credits for their initiatives.

Once a school or class commits to exploring and studying their watershed a wealth of interdisciplinary curriculum comes into play. Have the students do background research in addition to their field trip excursions. What animals used to live in this watershed? What species still do? Have any species been lost or impacted by human development? If so to what extent has their former range been restricted?

What is the history of human settlement in your watershed? What indigenous peoples

A watershed walk-about project leads students outside the classroom where decision making is no longer teacher-led, but draws students more fully into the democratic process. In the course of their research students may meet government officials, local business people and many members of the community, including the conservation community. Exposure to different viewpoints teaches them how to examine all sides of a complex issue. It helps them learn to differentiate between opinion and fact.

Ultimately, a watershed study program should lead students to a growing awareness that every thing living within the watershed is a neighbor, with as much right to the neighborhood as any human. It should also lead to a profound sense of belonging and caring with stewardship programs springing forth from the student's own initiatives. Cleaning garbage from a river or stream, educating the neighborhood to stop discharging toxic waste into waterways, tree planting to stabilize eroded slopes, and reintroducing fish to restored waterways, are just a few of the many stewardship activities schools worldwide have engaged in.

To help your students more fully understand the relationship between today's actions and tomorrow's consequences, have them compile a list of personal actions they can take to safeguard their watershed. It is best if they come up with, and commit to, their own actions, but here's a few examples:

- Never dump chemicals, paint, bleach or other toxic substances down drains.

- Volunteer to stencil messages on storm drains to remind people that the soap, oil and chemicals that enter them end up in streams, rivers and coastal shorelines that fish and other aquatic life depend on.

- Clean up pet waste after you walk your dog. Fecal matter enters waterways with heavy rain, polluting them and posing health hazards to fish, wildlife and humans.

- Reduce energy consumption in your home and school to reduce the likelihood of more hydro electric projects. Dams destroy the natural flow of rivers and devastate fish and wildlife habitat.

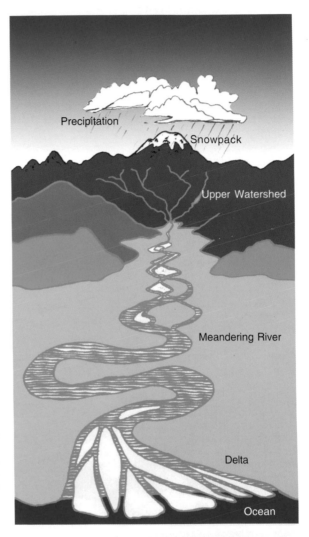

Precipitation

Snowpack

Upper Watershed

Meandering River

Delta

Ocean

- Remove garbage from culverts where water flows under roadways as this may block the passage for migratory fish. When doing river clean-ups, however, do not remove fallen trees and limbs from a waterway as these provide critical shelter for fish.

- Never remove trees, shrubs or natural ground cover from stream and river banks. This vegetation protects the embankment and helps to shade and cool the waterway making it more suitable for fish.

- Never drive all-terrain vehicles (ATVs) through streambeds as the weight of the vehicle can crush developing fish eggs in the gravel, and increase sedimentation which is detrimental to fish and other aquatic life.

- Refrain from using artificial fertilizers, herbicides, pesticides and insecticides on gardens and lawns. Heavy rain transports these toxic substances to waterways where they can be detrimental to life far downstream.

Wolf & Deer

Age Level: any age (6 and up)
Skills/Subject Areas: P.E., energy burner, group bonding
Eco-Concept:
> **Interdependence -** all things are connected to and depend on other living things

Required Materials: none
Prep Time: none

Description:

This is a good ice breaker activity for a group just getting to know one another, and before moving on to more complex exercises.

Let everyone find a partner and stand with that person by locking arms together side-by-side. Each of these two-person teams should be encouraged to spread out over the play area so as to create a maze for others to run between.

Once everyone has partnered up and positioned themselves, select one team to start the game. One of the players chosen becomes a 'wolf' pursuing the other – a frightened 'deer'. The deer player can only run for ten seconds before they must attach to another team of players by locking their arm with one of them. The one on the end, furthest from the deer player, must now break free to become the new 'deer.'

If a wolf player successfully tags a deer player, they immediately reverse roles; the 'deer' becomes the new 'wolf', and the 'wolf' becomes the 'deer.' If the new deer player does not link up with a team of players quickly, they risk being tagged back, and returning to their role as 'wolf'.

Kids will play this game until they're completely tuckered out. Have a brief discussion after the game, while they're catching their breath, to discuss the predator/prey interactions of wolves and deer.

- Did anyone use evasive tactics, like suddenly changing directions, which a deer might use in avoiding a wolf?

- Did faster runners tend not to get tagged at all? Do you think there's a survival advantage for deer being 'fleet-of-foot'?

- What other adaptations do deer have that allows them to escape or avoid predators like wolves?

- How does the social structure of a wolf pack help it when hunting deer, moose or elk?

Wolf Pack Territory

Age Level: any age (6 and up)
Skills/Subject Areas: science, cooperative learning, team building, group bonding, relationships in Nature, engaging the senses
Eco-Concepts:
   Interdependence - all things are connected to and depend on other living things
   Community - animals and plants live together in special areas that meet their needs
   Adaptation - everything has evolved to fit how and where it lives
Required Materials: scent markers
Prep Time: low- less than 10 minutes
Classroom Adaptations/Variations: research territorial behavior in social animals

Description:

Wolves maintain rigidly controlled territories by urinating at key scent markers on their range perimeters. As no two wolves have the same urine scent, these boundaries are easily distinguished. To simulate this situation for humans, bottled oils may be used. Garlic, lemon and peppermint oils are easily distinguishable, and can be purchased in small, portable bottles from any supermarket spice section.

The instructor uses three different scented oils to secretly mark out the edges of the three make-believe wolf territories. Large rocks, fallen trees, open earth patches, or tree trunks all make for likely scent sites. When daubed with the scented oils, these markers take on a very realistic look indeed. Do not overlap the wolf territories when laying out the boundaries; ideally, all 'packs' should be in distinct view of one another while playing the game. A total circumference of fifty meters is usually adequate for each 'pack's' territory.

There should be only one or two scent markers for every participant playing the game, and none of the youngsters should have any idea that the area has been marked out beforehand.

Divide the players into three equal-sized 'packs,' and scent the ankle of the largest boy in each group. Have the 'packs' get familiar with their 'pack scent' by sniffing the ankle of their 'alpha male'. Some discussion of the wolf's highly organized social structure, centering on a dominant male and a dominant female, might be in order. "A dominant wolf holds its tail high, stands stiff-legged, and bristles its mane," the instructor comments. "In its presence, a subservient animal cowers on the ground with its ears back, or stands with its tail between its legs." Encourage the participants to act out their social positions, then kneel and rehearse howling as a pack so that each individual is familiar with the distinct call of his or her group. Wolf howling may be a 'song fest' for sheer enjoyment or a way of warning other packs to keep away from occupied territory.

Give careful instructions to each 'pack' to search out the edge of their territory by sniffing. When an individual 'wolf' has located the correct scent, they are to kneel at that site and howl until all other members in their 'pack' are doing the same at a scent marker of their own. If an individual gets confused trying to locate their scent marker, they must search out their 'alpha male' to get another sniff of his ankle.

When all players of a 'pack' have located a scent marker and are kneeling and howling wildly, the 'alpha male' will now be able to determine the centre of his territory. All 'wolves' in the 'pack' are to immediately join him there for a great community howl. The first 'pack' howling loudly in unison from the exact centre of their range will be declared the dominant 'pack'.

Creating Your Own Curriculum

Integrating various subject areas into lessons and activites allows students to realize that no area of study stands on its own. For example, it's difficult to teach literature without at least mentioning the social context in which the author was writing. By the same token a study of science almost always touches upon the social values and economics that drive research and real world application.

Environmental education is the perfect cross disciplinary subject since it may encompass everything from art, social studies, physical education, literature, science and almost any topic teachers desire to incorporate into their lessons.

Following are a few examples to inspire the reader to realize that when it comes to creating a fresh and truly integrated curriculum through environmental education the teacher is only limited by their own creativity.

Creating a GREEN Center

Into the woods

Children seem to have a natural curiosity about things outdoors. Just take a crying infant outside and watch how quickly the fresh air, natural sounds and visual stimuli tend to calm them. As they grow up they are eager to run outside and uncover mysteries and investigate secrets of the forest, the beach, a meadow or pond. Anyone that has ever been fortunate enough to spend time hiking or camping with children surely knows this.

Important aspects of a suitable outdoor classroom are that it is safe and easily accessible. An outdoor classroom can be as simple as a small garden, flower bed, or vacant lot near the school. On the other hand it may also be as large as a state park or national forest.

Once a site is identified, study areas should be determined. This is when the fun and exploration begins!

Tying it All Together

Studying the environment naturally falls into the realm of science. However, with a little creativity educators can incorporate an almost endless variety of lessons in any subject area as a vehicle to increase enthusiasm and knowledge of the outdoors.

Below are only a few examples of how an educator may achieve a truly multi-disciplinary approach to teaching and learning in an outdoor classroom.

English as a Second Language

For teaching English as a Second Language (ESL), an outdoor classroom has great potential for fun and learning. A simple first ESL lesson may be a scavenger hunt using new vocabulary associated with a forest.

Prepare for the lesson by discussing things that might be seen or heard. Then provide a list of vocabulary to be read aloud and spelled correctly. Next, go outside and see if you can find examples of the new vocabulary.

You will be surprised how students become incredibly excited about their learning! In fact, you might not be able to keep up with their enthusiasm for the new worlds they discover and the new vocabulary they want to learn.

The context for the lesson is automatically set by being on the trail. The communicative opportunities are numerous and students will find it natural to attempt to communicate what they see, feel and hear. Take time to enjoy the magic of seeing a lizard basking in the sun or a butterfly fluttering around your head.

After the initial visit to the outdoor classroom make sure to plan several more excursions to reinforce and expand vocabulary as well as sharpen observation skills. The next step will be to write and illustrate stories about what the students witnessed on the trail.

Elementary Classroom

Students may practice observation, classification and writing skills by studying small plots on the forest floor. The teacher may decide to predetermine study plots ahead of time (see *Digital Decomposition pg.56*) or carry 'portable' study plots (see *Bigfoot pg.38*).

Next, students visit the plots to make and record their observations. Initial visits serve to orient the students to their assignment and introduce them to observation techniques.

Weekly trips to the outdoor classroom reinforce the idea that Nature is dynamic.

Don't be surprised if you notice a change in your students' attitudes or behavior while outdoors. The expressions on their faces when they encounter Nature in its many forms - a bird lands nearby, a monkey or squirrel scurries from limb to limb, or even the discovery of an ant highway - is priceless. It's those moments that inspire us. Those are the moments we strive for.

High School Science

Science is a natural extension of study for an outdoor space. The ability to enhance learning through practical experiences is the strength of formal lessons learned in the field. By using the space provided by an outdoor learning area science can be brought much more to life.

A wide array of topics including: topographic mapping, weathering and erosion, soil profiles, and rock and mineral identification; and any of the various disciplines such as botany, entomology or ecology may be studied outdoors. By combining the content of a high school course with the experience of Nature, students bridge the gap between the subject content and real life experiences.

While in an outdoor classroom, students learn how to observe and define relationships and then reflect and write about their experiences. This approach serves as a powerful tool for learning and often leaves a lasting impression on a young mind. A profound experience while learning outdoors illustrates the necessity and power of outdoor experiences in the education of global citizens.

Social Studies or History

The availability of water, plants and migratory routes of animals are integral to human history. It is possible to incorporate ideas and conduct studies to determine the types of economically important plants and animals found in a local area.

An opportunity for a truly integrated approach to learning presents itself when students learn that the science of plant identification and human uses of plants overlaps with the economics and history of human settlement and exploration.

The same is true for the study of animals since humans have often settled near fishing and hunting grounds as well as initiated exploratory expeditions for new sources of food and water.

Use these facts as discussion starters for research to be conducted in the outdoor classroom.

Art

Any naturalist and observer of the natural world will need artistic skills to sketch, label and identify the organisms they witness. Art conducted outdoors may also serve to feed the creativity in a student that cannot be unlocked in the confines of a walled classroom.

What better way to inspire creativity or nurture artistic ability than in a natural setting.

Incorporate art into almost any lesson by asking students to record their experiences and feelings by photographing, sketching or painting something which inspired them on the trail.

Poetry

Poetry lessons conducted outdoors often lead to avenues of creation, inspiration and expression that cannot be matched in an ordinary classroom. See *Poetry and Nature pg.136* on ways to incorporate poetry into almost any lesson conducted in Nature.

Go out and do it!

Once an outdoor classroom is established and used in lessons both students and instructors will find it exciting and rewarding to visit the outdoors as often as possible. Lessons learned and experienced directly will certainly leave lasting impressions and create fond memories of going outdoors and exploring the endless beauty of Nature.

Not only are outdoor classrooms invaluable teaching and learning tools, they can also inspire and build community. See the section on *Beautifying a Bombay Byway (pg.206)* which was directly inspired by a GREEN Center outdoor classroom built in Malaysia.

Eco-Olympics

A Multi-Task Adventure Race

With the huge success of many multi-sport adventure races like the Amazing Race and Eco-Challenge seen on TV, students will immediately relate to a similar event an instructor may suggest.

However, what makes the Eco-Olympics unique as an environmental education lesson is that it not only tests speed, strength and endurance, but also connects students to their surroundings and environment.

Eco-Olympics is an incredibly fun activity with a lot of room for variation and adaptation. In a sense, it serves as a prime example of how instructors can cross curriculum and integrate environmental education into almost any subject, even PE!

The Eco-Olympics is best run if the participants have had the opportunity to 'train' for the race for a few days or weeks. They can train athletically for the physical challenge ahead, but they will also need to prepare mentally by studying the flora and fauna of their local landscape or the components of environmental education that will be incorporated into the race.

Sample Events: plant, bird and fish identification; rock-climbing; swimming; team-challenge (such as *Save the Earth - pg. 28*); and a mystery event (such as *Mystery Critters - pg. 79*). Keep in mind you can mix and match or create new events based on the space you have access to and the local environment.

Setting it up:

One way to make Eco-Olympics fun is to schedule it as a culminating event to finish out the year, much like the traditional field day celebrated at many American schools. This gives participating students the opportunity to practice the skills and use the fitness they have acquired throughout the year in PE (i.e. climbing, swimming).

Work with the PE teachers to decide the logistics, timing, events and set-up of the race several months prior to the students being informed. Of course, SAFETY should always be a primary concern. It is a good idea for the instructors to run the course themselves prior to the event to clear any obstacles or adapt the activities in relation to safety considerations.

The Race:

A sample Eco-Olympics may include:

EVENT 1: 'Jungle Run'.
Students run through an outdoor classroom while identifying pre-marked plants along the way. Instructors should provide a list of possible plants that will be marked on the trail during the race.

A crucial step to learning about and identifying the plants is to see real, living specimens. By doing this, students can touch and identify distinguishing characteristics such as shape and smell. A trip to the activity site for study time prior to the event will help students sharpen their plant identification skills.

EVENT 2: 'Fish Identification' while snorkeling in the swimming pool.

An excellent way to incorporate an aquatic component in an urban environment with no easy access to clean lakes, rivers or streams, is to use a swimming pool. Laminated pictures of local fish and other aquatic fauna can be placed at the bottom of the pool using weights. Educational plastic marine-life figures also work well for this exercise.

During the race, students will swim down to identify as many fish species as possible and report back to a team mate at the poolside who records the information.

EVENT 3: 'Rock Climbing'.

Rock climbing is the ultimate test of endurance and stamina. Combine this with identification of karsts and cliff flora and fauna and you've got a stimulating event to challenge students in many ways!

Tying it all together:

Eco-Olympics is a highly adaptable event that can be conducted in many ways.One approach is to have co-ed teams of four players. Each team member is given a specific task (i.e. botanist, swimmer, rock climber and belayer).

The Eco-Olympics should begin at the location of the first event. The botanist speeds through the running trail as fast as they can while recording names of the pre-marked plants on a score sheet.

As they exit the trail they pass the score sheet on to the swimmers. The swimmers then sprint to the pool, put on their masks and jump in to identify the fish at the bottom. Once they have identified the fish, the swim up to the surface and relay the information to their teammate who records this. Swimmers repeat this until they have identified as many fish as possible.

Upon completing the task, they exit the pool and pass the score sheet to the climber/

belay team. The climbers then sprint to the climbing wall, put on their harnesses, get checked for SAFETY by a race official (PE teacher) and ascend the wall to a marked spot, identifying cliff species along the way. Once they reach the top, the clock is stopped and their time is recorded by a race official. The official also checks the accuracy of the team's plant and fish identifications and deducts minutes from their time based on the number of correct answers.

Deducting minutes from their time based on proper plant and animal identification ensures that the fastest team does not always win. In order to have the best time and win the race, students must learn their plants and fish well and strategize on how much time to dedicate to each identification activity.

Once the race is over you will find that students are exuberant and excited about doing it again!

A Multi-Discipline Day at a Beaver Pond

Imagine turning a natural community of plants and animals into a classroom that incorporates all of the major disciplines of a school curriculum in the course of a single day. Seashores, forests, mountain meadows, glacier valleys, rivers, lakes, deserts, bogs, grasslands, or even smaller microhabitats, can suffice for this exercise.

Just getting the students out in Nature, opening their senses to its infinite sounds, sights, smells and textures should be reward enough. But such novel, "out-of-the-box" approaches to education have also been shown to leave the most lasting impressions.

Consider something as simple as studying a beaver pond. Many areas of North America and Europe (where the species has been re-introduced) have beaver ponds in the countryside not too far from urban centers. Beaver dams and lodges are most often found in national, state, provincial, regional or county parks where human developments have not destroyed their habitat.

It would be best to complete a beaver pond multi-disciplinary study over the course of several days, perhaps a weekend or overnight camp out in a park. But if time, staff and budget constraints don't allow, a simple day at a beaver pond will do.

You will need to inspect your study site beforehand to become familiar with the setting and identify any and all possible hazards. Teachers of the various disciplines will also need to decide upon a strategy to conduct their lessons. Rotating small groups of students through various exercise stations, each led by the instructor best qualified in that field, would seem the most practical approach to take for a one-day study.

You will also need to take along a certain amount of equipment and personal supplies: binoculars, magnifying lenses, possibly a microscope, pH paper, fine mesh dip nets, plastic spoons and shallow basins, string marked off at 5-meter intervals, a detailed topographical map of the region, a compass, art paper and watercolors (chalk, pencils, crayons or felt pens), note pads, pens, calculators, clipboards and field guides to birds, mammals, fish, reptiles, amphibians and invertebrates. Students need to personally prepare themselves with: hats, sunscreen, sunglasses, rain gear or umbrellas, rubber boots (or runners/sandals that can get wet), insect repellent, a good healthy lunch, snacks and plenty of drinking water.

A bit of preparatory work in the classroom is a good idea as well, so that the students are already aware of and focused on their tasks when they arrive at the site. Use good sense in setting up the study stations. A writing assignment is going to be best conducted under the shade of trees on a sunny day, while more physically active exercises can take place almost anywhere in the vicinity of the pond. It's not a bad idea to erect a tarp between trees that can serve as a supply center, picnic lunch site, and as an emergency shelter in the event of a sudden rainstorm.

Below is a list of disciplines, assignments, briefing notes, and questions to stimulate discussion, suited to a beaver pond study. Use your own imagination to create more ideas and applications of these principles to other types of habitat.

SCIENCE: Biology, Botany and Chemistry

Wildlife Inventory

This is the most exciting and obvious place for students to start before too much activity and footprints begin to obliterate subtle wildlife signs and animal tracks along the shore and adjacent trails. Have the students set off in pairs as investigative detectives trying to pick up every clue of wildlife in the area. Beaver-cut trees, a lodge and dam should top their list, but as they gradually hone their observation skills they should detect far more subtle signs: the faint track of a muskrat in the mud, a fern tip nibbled by a passing deer, rabbit droppings hidden in the dry leaves along a trail, a well-camouflaged bird nest or spider web, a cluster of wiggling tadpoles at the pond's edge, a turtle sunning on a log, or the fast flutter of a female dragonfly depositing her eggs on the surface of the water.

Question: Has the alteration of this environment by the beaver increased or decreased the area's biodiversity? Give examples to support your argument.

(Notes: Beaver dams located at the headwaters of major streams stabilize flow, prevent stream bed erosion, create trout ponds, and improve habitat for many forms of wildlife. They are considered Nature's great conservationists)

Macro-invertebrate Study

This exercise offers insights into animals that students rarely ever see. Use dip nets along the edge of the pond to scoop up mollusks, aquatic worms, water bugs, dragonfly nymphs and a great range of other macro-invertebrates (animals with no spines). You can repeat this exercise in the creek that feeds into or drains the beaver pond to see how different the animals are in these different habitats. Look under the leaves of water lilies, the bottom side of rocks in the creek or pond to find other hidden wonders.

You will need a good macro-invertebrate book or chart to help the students identify the specimens they find. A shallow plastic basin, half-filled with pond water, can be used to keep specimens alive and well for study until they are released back into their waterway. Plastic spoons will hold enough water for many of these species to be observed closely under a magnifying lens.

Question: Based on your animal survey and macro-invertebrate study, would you say this watercourse is in a healthy state? If not, why?

Chemical Analysis

Give teams of students a pH kit and have them determine the pH of the water at the inflow to the lake, the pond itself, and the outflow. Is there a difference?

Question: Why might beaver ponds increase water acidity?

Forest Composition

Inventory the biodiversity of tree and shrub species surrounding the beaver pond esti-
mating percent of total coverage by each species (a field guide to local trees and shrubs will be essential).

Questions: Which species of trees do beavers prefer to cut in this region? Which do they clearly avoid? Can you think of some reasons for this?

(Notes: Beavers prefer poplar, trembling aspen, willow and birch but avoid coniferous trees that gum up their teeth.)

Environmental Impacts

Have the students survey the vicinity of the beaver pond carefully to determine if this is a relatively new or a long established site.

Questions: Based on available wood supply of preferred tree species, and how frequently beavers seem to be cutting trees, how long can this family of beavers continue to live here? What is the total area of land they flooded with the creation of their dam? How might this have impacted other species? How might it have improved habitat for others?

(Notes: A family of 5-6 beavers will require half a hectare of dense poplar, willow, birch or aspen trees for one winter's food supply.

As trees are cleared back from the pond's edge, the animals will forage 125 meters or more inland in their selective logging operations.)

Evolution

Provide a few good photos or drawings of beavers as students are unlikely to see these shy animals with so much activity around the site. Study the beaver's morphology.

Questions: What evolutionary adaptations do beaver display that make them such superb aquatic animals, powerful swimmers and tree fallers? Why do beaver incisor teeth continue to grow throughout their lives? What would happen if a beaver was held in captivity with no wood to gnaw on?

(Notes: Beavers have eyes with a transparent membrane that allow them to see well underwater. Both nostrils and ears can be closed when submerging, and the animal's lips can close behind the incisors allowing beavers to gnaw on twigs while underwater. The beaver's flat muscular tail, up to 30cm long and 18cm wide, serves as a powerful four-way rudder to propel them through water. On land the tail acts as a prop when the animal is sitting or standing upright, and serves as a counter balance when a beaver must walk on hind legs while carrying building materials like mud, stones and branches in its front paws. Beavers have exceptionally long, sharp incisors that grow continuously and are hardened with orange enamel on the forward face. As the upper and lower incisors are ground against each other, the outer tips of these teeth are maintained chisel-sharp.)

Fur Trade History

Sitting in the quiet shade of the forest surrounding the beaver pond, discuss the role that the fur trade played in exploration of the New World. Use a map of North America to show how early fur trade routes followed long-established trade routes of indigenous tribes. These overland trails later became the preferred travel routes for settlers and, in many cases, part of today's highway network.

(Notes: It is hard to imagine any animal that has influenced a nation's history to the extent that the beaver *Castor canadensis* has influenced the history of Canada and the USA. When Europeans began to settle in North America, beavers were the lure that drew them further and further into the wilderness.)

Questions: What countries actually fought wars in North America over fur trading territory? What companies dominated this industry? Which of these companies are still operating to this day?

The D'Orsay 1820   The Regent

Cultural Anthropology

In the same forest glade, challenge your students to imagine what life might have been like here 500 or more years ago. Discuss the daily lifestyle of the native people living here at that time and in what ways a beaver pond might have benefited them.

Discuss how fashion trends can effect wildlife populations. Consider the top hat craze in Europe that was made from the felt of pulverized beaver fur. The fashion craze was such that much of North America was without beavers during the first half of the 20th century.

Questions: In what ways did indigenous peoples utilize the beaver? What is a beaver "blanket?" Did the trade in beaver pelts benefit or impact upon indigenous peoples in North America?

(Notes: During the peak of the fur trade era more than 200,000 beaver pelts a year were sold to the European market for felt top hats. A large adult beaver skin – a 'blanket' – yielded enough fur for 18 hats.)

Physical Geography

Locate the beaver pond on a detailed topographical map of the area using a compass and surrounding features in the landscape for reference points.

Questions: Why might your study pond not show on a detailed topographical map of the region? When was your map printed? How old do you suspect this pond is? What geographical features influenced the beaver to build a dam at this location?

Set up a compass course connecting the beaver dam to various tree-cutting sites and back to the lodge for students to test their orienteering skills.

Question: Do you suppose the nocturnally active beavers have courses of their own they follow at night? (Look for evidence both on the land and at the edge of the water).

MATH: Physics, Geometry and Algebra

Water Volume

Determine the volume of water held back by the beaver dam by measuring the circumference of the pond with your string (marked at 5-meter intervals) and determining the average depth of the pond. (Note: You will need a rowboat, canoe or inflatable raft and a string with a sinker weight to get a series of soundings)

Questions: What features influence water volume in a beaver pond? What is the minimum depth of water required for beavers to access their winter supply of food under the ice?

(Notes: Beavers in northern latitudes, where ponds freeze over, must construct food piles underwater to sustain them in winter. Each such cache is an accumulation of the beaver's favorite food items gathered in the autumn and placed in deep water close to the lodge or bank den.)

Rate of Flow

Determine the rate of flow of the creek exiting the pond and calculate how long it would take to drain the pond if there was no inflow.

Question: Why do beavers respond instinctively with more sticks and mud to the sound of running water?

Basic Physics

Take a critical look at the beaver dam and lodge from an engineering point of view. Survey the shoreline for cut trees and inventory what percent of them were felled in the direction of the pond.

Questions: Why is a beaver dam much wider at the base than at the top? What is the angle of repose of the dam and the lodge? Why do most trees that beavers cut along shore fall towards the water? Are they really such skilled tree fallers?

(Notes: There are many myths about beavers, such as the one that credits the animal with the intelligence to fell a tree in a chosen direction with the expertise of a lumberjack. The simple truth is, a beaver has no idea which way a tree is going to fall; many get hung up and some even fall atop the beaver. Stream bank trees tend to fall towards water because shoreline erosion has already tilted them in that direction.)

LANGUAGE ARTS:

In a peaceful forest setting near the beaver pond, challenge students studying foreign

---

Calculating the volume of water in a lake

In order to calculate how much water is in a lake use the following method:

Equipment needed:
Length of rope, measuring tape (100m or more), canoe/boat (optional), rope with a weighted end and calibrated at 1m intervals (for measuring depth), paper, pencil

REMEMBER: The more measurements you take, the more accurate your estimation will be!

1) Measure or estimate the length (l) of the lake at several evenly spaced intervals.
2) Measure or estimate the width (w) of the lake at several evenly spaced intervals.
3) Measure the depth (d) of the lake using the weighted and calibrated rope.
4) Calculate the average length.
5) Calculate the average width.
6) Calculate the average depth (from surface to bottom).
7) Multiply l * w * d to determine volume.

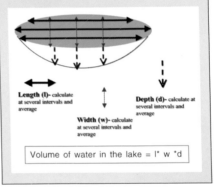

Length (l)- calculate at several intervals and average

Width (w)- calculate at several intervals and average

Depth (d)- calculate at several intervals and average

Volume of water in the lake = l * w *d

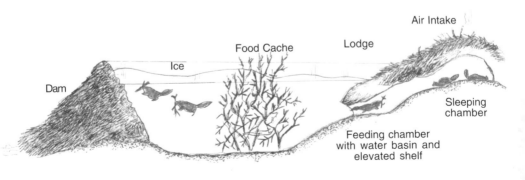

Air Intake

Food Cache

Lodge

Ice

Dam

Sleeping chamber

Feeding chamber
with water basin and
elevated shelf

languages to describe in that language: 1) the beauty of the physical setting, 2) the methods by which beavers construct dams and lodges, 3) the distinguishing physical features of a beaver.

Questions: What language did the aboriginal peoples that first occupied this area speak? Why was trade jargon developed between European traders and North American native peoples? What languages did the European traders that competed fiercely for trading rights speak?

FINE ARTS: Art, Music and Theater

Drawing & Painting

Using oils, watercolors, crayons, felt pens, pencil or charcoal, draw or paint a scene from the beaver pond: 1) as a naturalist with careful attention to physical detail, 2) as an impressionist, romancing the scene, or 3) in an abstract, like a Picasso. Have the students compare their masterpieces.

Question: If no two humans look upon a landscape in quite the same way, do you suppose it's even more different for animals?

On the reverse side of each students drawing, or another art paper, challenge them to draw the beaver pond as viewed: 1) by a bird flying overhead, 2) a beaver swimming underwater, or 3) through the kaleidoscope eyes of a dragonfly.

Music

Encourage students to listen carefully to the sounds of Nature all around them - the wind in the reeds, the rustle of leaves, the courtship call of a bird, and the incessant chatter of insects. Using a musical score sheet challenge them to record this symphony using musical notes or phonetics. Have them imagine how completely different the overture would be during the night. You might even want to challenge your music class to compose a symphony based on the sounds during a day in the life of a beaver pond.

Questions: What instruments could be employed to mimic early morning bird calls, the drone of insects at mid day, an orchestra of night frogs, katydids and crickets? What instrument could mimic the falling of a beaver-cut tree, or the slap of a beaver tail sending out a warning across the water?

Theater

Have students select their own roles for an improvisation in the woods. They can come up with their own idea for a short play, or expand on one of the following concepts:

1) The utter amazement of the first Europeans to set eyes on the North American beaver, and the challenge of trying to report this discovery to a disbelieving public back in Europe.

2) A beaver family snug in their lodge for the winter, but a bit put out with having to share the space with free loading muskrats that have contributed nothing to the lodge's construction or maintenance.

3) A passionate environmentalist engaged in a debate with a grizzled old trapper who opens with the argument: "How can you eco-nuts love a beaver and hate a dam?"

HEALTH

Using comprehensive field guides to edible and medicinal plants, have students set out in teams to identify as many edible plants, teas and natural medicines as they can find in the vicinity of the beaver pond.

Questions: Which plants would be good sources of Vitamin C, carbohydrates and essential oils? If humans discovered aspirin in the bark of willow trees, do you suppose this pondside plant is used medicinally by beavers and other animals?

BELONGING

"I thought the Earth remembered me,
She took me back so tenderly.
Arranging her dark skirts, her pockets full of lichens,
I slept as never before..."

Annie Dillard
Pilgrim at Tinker Creek

INTROSPECTIVE ACTIVITIES

Some of the best lessons on the trail can be experienced during the few instances when students get to sit quietly, contemplate life and simply take in whatever is around them. Teachers are sometimes so caught up in getting the information into a student's brain and copied into their notebooks that they don't have the time or take the time to get to know their deeper thoughts and feelings. Many of these lessons have very little structure and are intentionally left 'open' for the participant to interpret however they like.

The following are examples of the types of activities that can lead to a deeper level of connection with both the self and Nature.

Spirit Spot

People with Western secular biases find it difficult to imagine a place imbued with power, much less suited to a specific individual. North American indigenous peoples recognized the special powers that could come to a person by placing oneself in the right frame of mind and the right location. *Spirit Spot* tries to reintroduce youth to this experience, as well as provide a scheduled time for quiet introspection and intimate Nature observation every day.

For this exercise to be successful, a facilitator must prepare youngsters psychologically. Just sending them off alone each day can be too much like a "Go stand in the corner" punishment.

Tell the participants about the native traditions where youth their age would spend long periods alone in search of spirit guardians, and about the opportunity they will have every day to see the same place under different conditions — sunny, shady, windy, calm, wet, and foggy — and the many animals that might approach them if they're quiet: birds, chipmunks, squirrels, and deer. Above all, tell them that this exercise will help prepare them for their *Solo/ Vision Quest* should they ever choose to have an opportunity to spend twenty-four hours completely alone. (See pgs.147-148)

In finding *Spirit Spots,* a few rules must be observed: first, no individual should be in view of another, or in view of road traffic or buildings. Second, silence must be maintained at all times, so the experience is not ruined for others. Third, once a *Spirit Spot* has been chosen (in a forest, along a stream, or on the shoreline), the youngster is duty-bound to return to that same spot each day.

The leader must explain the signal for the end of the *Spirit Spot* — a conch-shell blast or loud drumbeat. Schedule this exercise early in the day, or in the evening near sunset. Reserve the same time period every day for this thirty to forty-five minute exercise. Don't make the Spirit Spot too short (or it will be meaningless), or too long (as some youngsters will complain of boredom). It may be necessary for facilitators to monitor participants at their *Spirit Spots* for the first few days or until a routine is established.

On the third or fourth day of the exercises, give all participants paper and watercolors, crayons, felt pens, or colored pencils. Ask them to try putting the images from their *Spirit*

Spot on paper. It needn't be a photographic image, perhaps just colors. Tell them to fully express themselves, as these paintings are confidential.

On the following day, give everyone a pen and paper and ask them to write a letter to themselves — "Dear Me." Ask them to express how they feel about their lives up to that point, how they feel to be there at their *Spirit Spot*, and what they imagine themselves to be like three years into the future.

The letters, strictly confidential, should close with a loving salutation and signature. Both the paintings and the letters should be sealed in an envelope, addressed to the youngster they belong to, and mailed out to them several months later.

Nature's Orchestra

How often do youth listen to, or even conceive of, the sounds of Nature as music? In a rock-till-you-drop culture, it is not easy to tune in to a frog orchestration at dusk, the babble of a brook under a snowbank, or the call of a thrush deep in the forest.

Nature's Orchestra helps put some people more in touch with the oldest music on Earth. Any natural setting will suit this activity, as long as it is well removed from human-generated noise.

Once a location is found, give each of the participants a large index card drawn up as a musical-score sheet, but without any notes on it. The participants spread out so that each is alone to record the music he or she hears all around.

At first, most will hear nothing. Then they may pick up on the more obvious sounds: the call of a raven, the chatter of a squirrel, the song of a bird, or the buzz of a bee. The subtle sounds will come more gradually: the whisper of wind in the treetops, the muffled creaking of a trunk, the murmur of a distant creek or seashore, or the scurry of a mouse through forest litter.

Whatever they hear, they are to record. Nature is the composer here, not the student. Those who have a grasp of music may wish to record musical notes on the bars of their score sheets. Others may find it easier to write out phonetically the sounds they hear: swish, swish, swish, swish. Bzzzz zzzzz...swish, chirp, chirp, ka-chirp.

Little drawings can be used to try distinguishing the source of different sounds. Even a color spectrum could be employed, ranging from cool to warm colors – blue waves for soft sounds to bold red slashes for loud sounds. The object here is to listen and express the auditory experience as creatively as possible on paper.

This is a very personal experience, perfect for a *Spirit Spot*. If any would like to share their score sheet with another, they should be encouraged to do so afterward. Otherwise the *Nature's Orchestra* sheets should be hidden away in each youngsters personally addressed envelope, along with their *Spirit Spot* drawing and Letter to the Future. (See pg.133) Months after they leave this special place, the sounds of their *Spirit Spot* can arrive in the mail.

Poetry and Nature

Often times students are asked to write a poem, a song, a rap, a rhyme or complete a piece of art in class. However, this task can take on another dimension when completed outdoors immersed in the landscape and surrounded by the sounds of birds, cicadas and the wind blowing through the trees.

Sit each student in a spot by themselves far away from friends and classmates. Assure them that you won't be too far away and you'll be listening for them and will return in a few minutes after they have had time to complete their task. Encourage the students to complete a poem, a song or a piece of art. Tell them to wait a few minutes before they start and take time to absorb the smells, listen to the sounds and feel the air around them.

Often the students will be so used to structured lessons that they ask, "How many lines does it have to be?", "Can it rhyme?", "Does it have to rhyme?" etc. Just assure them that there are no instructions and that it can be as long or short as they want. Their work can be a rhyme, a song or even a drawing. Tell them they can do whatever they feel like doing in regards to the assignment. The key to success, however, is to remain quiet and still for as long as possible so that they can be inspired.

As the teacher you should also complete the task and create a work of your own. After a sufficient amount of time has passed collect all the students and form a sharing circle. You might have to share your work first to encourage the students to share their own.

The end results are sometimes astounding. You may discover that your students have very deep and insightful thoughts and feelings. You may see another side of your students and allow them to see another side of you that isn't expressed in the confines of a classroom. This activity is often extremely rewarding for both students and teacher.

Give it a try and adapt it to your surroundings and students!

Forest Blankets

A classic acclimatization experience, *Forest Blankets* appeals to all, even hyperactive youth. *Forest Blankets* makes for a very nice closing to a forest outing, or as a resting period following a fast game like *Hungry, Hungry Marten.* (See pg.71)

Gather the group together in a forest area with soft moss, deep beds of needles, or leaves forming the forest floor. "We've had an opportunity today to touch, smell, taste, and see the forest in many different ways," the instructor begins, "but now we're going to totally become a part of this ecosystem. We're going to pretend that we are clumps of moss, branches, or leaves that have fallen from the canopy overhead to rest here on the forest floor. We will let our bodies melt into the earth, looking up at the treetops where we've come from, and reflect on what we will again become as we're recycled as nutrients back into the ground. There is no life and death here, only renewal," the instructor says. "Even the insects are part of the process, so try to relax if one should crawl onto you. Feel its tiny feet moving over your skin." (Apply insect repellent only if mosquitoes and other biting insects are especially annoying.)

Whispering now, the instructor lays down one of the youngsters on his or her back while all the others help half-bury the person under leaves, needles, branches, or moss. Put just enough weight on the body for the weight to be noticeable. Hands are especially important areas for direct contact with the forest litter. Try to set an arching branch over the person's eyes with enough leaves or needles on it to create a three dimensional effect when looking up. Also try to use only forest litter – not living specimens.

Once the first youngster is comfortably tucked away under a 'forest blanket', move on to a new location in silence, eight to ten meters away, and begin to bury the next volunteer. Eventually, everyone should be lying peacefully out of view of one another and staring up through the treetops.

There is no optimum time period for *Forest Blankets*. It depends totally on the group. Some will get restless after ten minutes; others will enjoy the experience for nearly an hour or more. Signs of fidgeting or talk should be the instructor's cue to end the exercise.

Pick the participants up in the order they were dropped off. Ask each to describe the experience. Many will talk of the animals they heard: squirrels, songbirds, woodpeckers. Some will have revelations: "Did you know that raindrops fall in spirals?"

One boy in particular had a most memorable experience. A mosquito landed on the moss above his eyes and spread its wings to dry in the sun. Looking through the wings of the mosquito to the treetops fifty meters up, the boy saw an eagle circling in the clearing overhead. Months later in school, an English teacher got to wonder about the title of an essay handed in: "Seeing the World through the Wings of a Mosquito."

Empowerment Pebbles

Native peoples have always recognized or imbued in animals certain human-like traits. While skeptics are quick to call this "anthropomorphism," the traits are easily recognized by youth. Certainly, otters appear to be playful, and squirrels assertive. No one questions the strength of a bear, the extraordinary expressions of a frog, or the patience of a spider. So what's wrong with seeing qualities in Nature that we'd like to develop in ourselves? Empowerment Pebbles do just that.

Have participant's select fourteen small, smooth pebbles from a shoreline or riverbank. (Be sure to take them from dry embankments so as not to disturb fish-spawning beds.) Use simple pictograph designs as models and let each youngster paint or draw (with waterproof felt pens) these designs on their rocks.

As the children are drawing a design on each pebble, tell them the special gift that each of these animals brings to them and ask them to think about how they can use that gift in their lives. Use animals that are native to your region and familiar to the youth. Examples:

Wolf – Self-Esteem: Just as the wolf howls its proud song to the moon, you too must recognize that you are a unique and special person. Give yourself some appreciation. Sing your own song, for you are a loveable and capable person!

Raven – Curiosity: The raven is never bored, always curious, always exploring every corner of the world. So too must you awaken your sense of wonder – discover the hidden miracles in life and immerse yourself in its endless wonders.

Salmon – Sharing: Just as the salmon shares its body with bear, otter, eagle and human, so too must you learn to share your food, your feelings, your fears and your dreams for the future. After all sharing is the most important tradition.

Spider – Patience: Spider spins her web and waits, and waits, and waits....Spider knows that her patience will be rewarded with a fly in her trap and a meal for her young. You must learn the lesson of patience; all things will not come to you instantly. Know patience and stay focused on your goal.

Bear – Inner Strength: The powerful grizzly bear brings you the gift of strength – inner strength to help you through weak moments in your life. Like the grizzly mother who overturns logs to feed insects to her cubs, or to protect them from danger, you too must use your physical strength appropriately.

Hummingbird – Joyfulness: Hummingbird, this joyful little spirit, brings happiness into your life. All the sweetness of the nectar in the flowers is yours. Remember to take time to smell the flowers and find joy in all you see and do.

Squirrel – Assertiveness: The squirrel knows when its personal territory is being invaded and scolds the intruder with its chatter. It does not harm the intruder, but lets everyone know what's going on. You too must know when to be assertive, to protect yourself from others acting against your own will.

Deer – Peacefulness: The gentle deer brings you the gift of a peaceful spirit. Deer are always aware, always alert, but at the same time they are peaceful and gentle. Take time in your life for the quiet pleasures; take a moment alone with your thoughts, in a beautiful meadow of wildflowers or the hushed silence of the forest, and you will know the gift of the deer.

Frog – Self-Expression: Frog brings you the gift of self-expression, for the frog sings songs for all the world to hear. Express yourself; if its not your destiny to sing like a lark, but to croak like a frog, then go ahead and do it – and with all your might. Make yourself heard!

Goose – Cooperation: Goose teaches us that when we share common direction with others, its best to cooperate because we'll get there quicker and easier traveling with the thrust of one another (like geese in a 'V' formation) than we will by travelling alone. Like the geese who honk from behind to encourage those up front to keep up their speed, give encouragement to others and you will be on the pathway to cooperation.

Mosquito – Tolerance: Life is full of little annoyances, like the mosquito who teaches us tolerance. Don't let the little things that bug you seem bigger than they really are. The tiny mosquito is there to remind us that our problems in life are not as great as we think.

Loon – Spirituality: The call of the loon from the glassy surface of a tranquil lake is a reminder for you to seek your inner spirit. Like the loon who occasionally dives below the surface of the water, your spirituality will at times feel distant. Let it resurface, just as the loon must return to the surface to sustain life.

Beaver – Self-Control: Beaver always knows when and where to act; the beaver hears water running through the dam and responds with more sticks and mud. You too must learn the lesson of self-control, to know when to take charge of circumstances affecting your life.

Eagle – Vision: Eagle flies high with incredible eyes. There is nothing eagle cannot see. So too must you have vision to know where you want to go in life – not just to see what's directly ahead, but to see beyond the visible. Keep your dreams close to your heart, for without a vision you perish.

Once all fourteen pebbles have been painted and the gift each animal has to offer is understood, have each youngster make a small basket or medicine pouch to keep them in. A small cloth or leather bag with a drawstring (like a marble bag) is easy to make. This will be each youngster's bag of *Empowerment Pebbles*. Every day, they are to close their eyes and randomly draw one pebble from the bag. This will be their special power, or focus, for the day. By keeping that day's pebble as a touchstone in their pockets, they will be reminded of their discipline throughout the day.

At the end of two weeks all pebbles will have been drawn and are then returned to the medicine bag to begin the ritual anew. Thus, twice a month each youngster has a special day to reflect on being joyful, patient, generous, cooperative, etc. The magic of using *Empowerment Pebbles* is that they allow youngsters, with all their worldly distractions, a private meditative moment each day.

Talking to the Trees

Native peoples consider trees to have strong healing powers. Native women still pray to the cedar tree before removing bark to weave hats, baskets, or make medicine.

"Look at me friend
I come to ask for your garment
You always take pity on us, for there is
nothing for which you cannot be used
Because it is your way
That there is nothing for which we cannot
use you,
For you are really willing to give us your
garment.
I come to beg you for this
Long Life Maker, Healing Woman,
Supernatural One
For I am going to make a basket for
berries out of you.
I pray friend, to tell your friends about
what I ask you
Take care friend, keep sickness away
from me Healing Woman,
Long Life Maker"

--Kwakiutl Prayer to Cedar Tree

For native people, trees came to symbolize the sacredness of all life, and they rested beside trees with a feeling of being close to a mothering power. The Pacific Northwest Coast natives believed that one's longevity could be increased by leaning against an ancient cedar tree. Twelve-hundred-year-old cedars can still be found living on this coast.

Talking to the Trees is an introspective exercise that helps youngsters gain insight into the close relationship with the land that all our ancestors once knew. This activity can take place any time of the day, but it will require some preparation on the part of a facilitator to set the right mood.

There are many poems and writings about trees and forests that can be read to help set the mood. Example:

"Trees seem to do their feats so effortlessly. Every year a given tree creates absolutely from scratch ninety-nine percent of its living parts. Water lifting up tree trunks can climb one hundred and fifty feet an hour; in full summer a tree can, and does, heave a ton of water every day. A big elm in a single season might make as many as six million leaves, wholly intricate, without budging an inch; I couldn't make one."

--Annie Dillard, **Pilgrim at Tinker Creek.**

Leave the child to listen to the heartbeat of the tree as well as their own. Words at this point may not be necessary at all.

A facilitator can never know whether or not any given participant actually found something to say to their tree, unless they feel like sharing their experience with others. Some may be more comfortable writing a poem or relating their feelings in their journals. Encourage them to take journals along. One boy wrote:

"Tall trees stretch to the sky
While in their shadows
The fallen empire lies to rot
Cool, dark and dim, the forest is alive
Green boughs match green moss
Red cedar matches red earth
The thousand year children reign today
And topple tomorrow."

Have the participants spread out through the forest so that no one is in view of another. When each finds a tree they like, they should sit down and lean against it, or embrace it standing. Some will find it easier to talk with their eyes closed. Trees are good listeners and can keep secrets forever, so there is no need to be shy.

To enhance this experience for the skeptic, take a stethoscope and position the youngster at a tree with thin bark. By listening carefully, one can hear the sap being drawn upward, much like a human heartbeat. (This is especially pronounced in the springtime.)

Earth in the Hand

It's hard for children to grasp the immense size of the Earth – more than 40,000 km in circumference. A child's world is so preoccupied with miniature things: toy cars and baby dolls, small animals and playhouses. Perhaps if the Earth could fit into the palm of a child's hand they'd learn early on what a fragile and precious gift it really is.

Earth in the Hand is a creative visualization exercise that requires a reflective mood and a setting where youngsters can quiet their minds and bodies. Sitting on a beach watching a sunset after a physically exerting game might be an appropriate time for this exercise. Sunset is the most reflective time of day. Campfires too lend themselves well to reflective moods. But candles in the dark have a special magic all their own, and it is in a candlelit meadow or forest glade in the dark of night that *Earth in the Hand* will leave its most lasting impression.

You can do this activity with something as simple as a round stone. Have participants explore a riverbank or rocky beach until they each find a beautiful round stone, one that's small enough to fit easily into their hands.

Tell them not to worry if the stone isn't perfectly round; the world isn't either – there's a bulge at the equator 43.2 km wider than the circumference at the North and South Poles due to the centrifugal force created by the Earth's rotation.

Instead of using stones, you may want to create a miniature Earth out of clay, firing and glazing (or painting) it. This is a good project for school groups and can be incorporated into larger lessons on the Earth itself. Statistics on the Earth can be obtained from an encyclopedia or from websites, and can broaden the educational component of this exercise. Such statistics can include the circumference of Earth (40,024 km), surface area (316,778,856 square km) and highest and lowest temperatures. Remind the participants, whether they choose rock or clay for their miniature Earth, that the material is a partial microcosm of the Earth itself.

Once youngsters have created, or selected, their own miniature world, have them carry it in their pocket for a day or two as a touchstone. On the night of the exercise, everyone carries their 'Earth' in a candlelit procession to the pre-selected site in the forest or meadow. Songs can be sung or chanted during the procession under the stars; this is a ritual to honor the Earth.

Find a comfortable place for everyone to sit in a circle while holding their candles. "We're going to blow out the candles now and experience the black void of space," the instructor begins. Some flute music can be played here to set the mood for the creative visualization that follows.

"Now hold your 'Earth' in your open palms close to your heart," the leader continues. "Close your eyes and breathe in very slowly. Hold the breath for a moment and feel yourself relax as you exhale very slowly." This is repeated three times. Each time, the leader speaks slowly and softly, telling the youngsters how each part of their body is relaxing deeper and deeper. When the entire group is in a very deep state of relaxation, the leader draws on an image to

be etched in each child's mind. "Just imagine if the Earth were only the size of the stone you hold in your hand – what a totally awesome object it would be. People from all over would come to marvel at this incredible treasure of yours. They would watch in awe as thin veils of water suspended in gas enveloped the ball – clouds always shifting, forever changing shape, flowing pink and lavender, crimson and burning orange with the setting sun. Clouds that create ever-changing windows to the Earth below, never revealing this brilliant gem in quite the same way.

"People would be spellbound by the fire, molten rock, and gases that spew violently

from the centre of this ball. They would wonder how anything so beautiful and seemingly fragile could be so dynamic and alive. If the viewers looked very, very closely, they would be staggered by the number of creatures that live on the surface of your stone – creatures that swim and those that fly, four-legged and two-legged wonders that roam the land from the snow-crowned mountains to the deepest canyons in the sea.

"In time, people would come to love and cherish this irreplaceable sphere. They would declare it sacred because it was the only one. They would pray to it and seek healing from it, for it would represent a miracle like no other. And people would defend it with their lives for they would come to know that their lives would be nothing without it. If this wondrous world were only the size of the 'Earth' you hold in your hand."

Flute music is again played while all in the group are asked to keep their eyes closed. "Now imagine that you are that magical sphere and it is you," the leader begins again. "Slowly tilt your head skyward and open your eyes. The wonder of the firmament is that, as far as we have been able to determine, you are the only object out there that is known to support life....

Make a promise to yourself here tonight, with the stars as your witnesses that you will always care for this symbolic Earth in your hand and keep it close to your heart, as you will the larger Earth that this represents."

A moment of silence here is followed by the leader relighting the candles and an intimate opportunity for each child to share his or her feelings and personal promises.

Talking Feather

Put a shy person in front of a group to speak, then watch their hands. Often the hands go into their pockets, up to fix their hair, over to wiggle a loose shirt button, and back into their pockets. But give the same person an object to hold while they speak and they can forget about what to do with their hands and concentrate more on what they want to say.

On *Rediscovery,* (See pgs.178-187) the object is endowed with power. "This is a talking feather," the leader tells the group around the fire on the first evening. "It is a very special feather because it will give you the power to speak. There are rules you must observe when holding this sacred feather. You and you alone may speak. You must speak from the heart and you must speak the truth. Always treat the feather with respect and pass it clockwise around the circle."

According to Haida Elders, such a system was used for group sharing from time beyond memory. Chiefs still hold a talking stick when addressing a group. Not all native groups can use eagle feathers in this man-

ner: to some the feather is so sacred that only a shaman may hold one. The Ute, Lakota and Pueblo peoples on Colorado's Rediscovery Four Corners pass a crystal rather than an eagle feather. Any object can be imbued with "talking powers" once the group recognizes it as such. The more natural and culturally appropriate the object is, the greater the powers it will possess.

The policy at many Rediscovery camps is that if a crisis occurs in camp or an individual is seriously troubled, anyone can call for the feather to be passed. Whatever activity is underway at that time – be it a meal, a hike, group game, or workshop – will be stopped immediately. Nothing is more important than an individual needing to express himself or herself through the feather. Participants have never been known to abuse this privilege.

One extremely important lesson for group leaders, sometimes learned the hard way, is to respect a person's silence. Group leaders can get so caught up in facilitating that at times they are tempted to try helping a youngster who holds the feather but can't find words to speak. A Haida Elder set everyone straight on that point: "A child's silence is as important a statement as any words spoken by any other child."

Begin with one 'talking' object and progress to a similar (but older or larger) object during the course of the program to help the group mark their personal development and growth. For instance, replace an immature eagle feather with an adult eagle feather or a small crystal with a larger rock when the staff feels that the group has really matured together. By marking such a progression, everyone has the new responsibility of the more advanced behavior or attitude toward each other. They can be reminded that they've all advanced to a higher level should any temporarily regress.

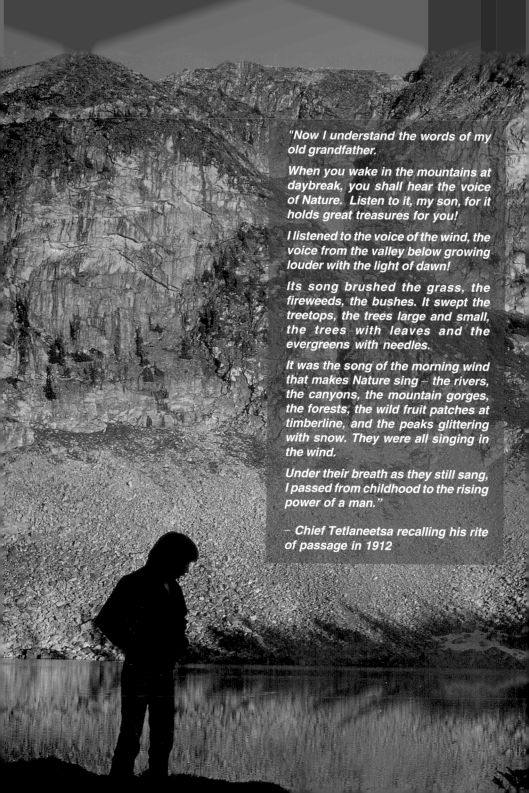

"Now I understand the words of my old grandfather.

When you wake in the mountains at daybreak, you shall hear the voice of Nature. Listen to it, my son, for it holds great treasures for you!

I listened to the voice of the wind, the voice from the valley below growing louder with the light of dawn!

Its song brushed the grass, the fireweeds, the bushes. It swept the treetops, the trees large and small, the trees with leaves and the evergreens with needles.

It was the song of the morning wind that makes Nature sing – the rivers, the canyons, the mountain gorges, the forests, the wild fruit patches at timberline, and the peaks glittering with snow. They were all singing in the wind.

Under their breath as they still sang, I passed from childhood to the rising power of a man."

– Chief Tetlaneetsa recalling his rite of passage in 1912

The Solo/Vision Quest

Vision questing has been the traditional rite of passage on the North American continent for thousands of years. Natives marked the transition from childhood to adulthood with long periods of isolation, fasting, and meditation in the wilderness in search of spirit guardians. Some native peoples still pursue vision quests as the highest form of Native American religion, held so sacred that it borders on heresy to mention the practice in this context. Mention is made merely to distinguish between the solo experience of many adventure programs and the more culturally attuned and spiritual focus of *Solo/Vision Quests*. Through the careful guidance of native Elders and spiritual leaders, participants can take part in a time-honoured rite of passage. The benefits of this traditional approach for youth in our time are so profound that the *Solo/Vision Quest* can become one of the greatest keys for unlocking the doors to self-discovery.

Buying cigarettes, graduating from high school, getting a driver's license, voting, being old enough to drink in bars or joining the army – these events mark the transition from childhood to adulthood in our Western society. Usually void of spirituality, they range over a number of years without any one event whereby a child becomes accepted as an adult. By contrast, tribal societies clearly distinguish this important stage in personal development.

Solo/Vision Quests resemble other solos in the sense that an individual stays alone in the wilderness for a twenty-four hour period with little food and other resources: water, two or three matches, a pen and paper for recording thoughts, a sleeping bag, and a cooking pot. But *Solo/Vision Quests* differ from most camp solos in some important ways. First, no participant is required to take part and no participant will be put down for not doing so. The achievement is far greater when one approaches it of one's own free will. Second, ceremonies marking the beginning and end of the Solo experience are in keeping with the traditions of the indigenous local culture and are, whenever possible, presided over by native Elders.

These might include food offerings on a fire to the ancestors who have gone before, smudging (smoke purifications with sweetgrass, sage, or cedar), pipe ceremonies (tobacco offerings to the sacred directions), and ceremonial sweat lodges for purification. Third, the entire camp connects in spirit with those on their Solos. The group lights a vigil fire during the ceremony just prior to the soloists' departure. Those remaining in camp take turns keeping a silent vigil by this fire throughout the twenty-four hour period. The vigil fire not only acts as a quiet reflective place for those not on solo, but also provides an important transition zone for those returning to camp either early (through unsuccessful attempts to stay out) or at the completion of their quest.

It is extremely important to prepare participants psychologically for the *Solo/Vision Quest*. Native Elders can be particularly effective in this regard, describing how children once did this when there were far more wild and dangerous animals than today. The late Wilfred Bennett, a Haida Elder, told a group of soloists, "If you can learn to live in harmony with this experience, it will carry over into the rest of your life."

Ironically, the younger a person is, the more likely they are to volunteer for a *Solo/Vision Quests* and the more likely they are to successfully complete it. What this suggests about confidence building as one grows older is the exact opposite of what one would expect.

Another strange irony occurs during solos. A group bully or the top of the "pecking order" will almost always fail to complete this experience. A native elder once explained it this way: "The reason a child acts that way is because he doesn't know or like himself. Nobody wants to spend that much time alone with someone they don't know or like."

Those deemed "least likely to succeed" most often return successfully from solos. Everyone wonders why the "tough guys," almost without exception, fail in their solos by coming back before dark. First impressions suddenly turn upside-down in youngsters' minds. A necessary humbling experience for some, restoring self-pride for others. Solo does a lot more than develop self-confidence: it connects youngsters directly with the Earth and themselves. A boy wrote of his experience with fire charcoal on his driftwood shelter: "Here I am on solo night. At first it gave me quite a fright but when I see the swaying trees and hear the peaceful rhythm of the sea, I feel more confident in me."

A word of caution. While the *Solo/ Vision Quest* is a profound experience and highly recommended activity, care must be exercised to ensure participant safety. Youngsters should never be located near natural hazards, e.g., avalanche slopes, grizzly bear trails or well-known feeding locations, below high-tide lines, near creeks that flash flood, or below a tree that might be inclined to drop a large branch. Knives and hatchets, the number-one cause of injury in these situations, should be forbidden – especially with younger children. Fires should only be part of a solo if all campers have been trained in proper fire building and safety and if forest-fire danger is extremely low or nil. Fires do help a lot of youngsters through the experience, as a poem by a young girl, Dana Nyehold, out on her solo, testifies:

"The firelight is dancing
and singing a beautiful song;
black, white, orange and red
carry me through
the dark hours I dread.
The long wispy puffs of smoke
are whispering welcome to all –
all alone with no company,
except my firelight dancers."

Note: All fire locations should be carefully selected by the instructor. Every participant's location should be recorded on a detailed map and a secret spot check should be made just prior to dark.

COMFORT ZONES

We all have invisible barriers between ourselves and our experiences. We carry these barriers around with us and plant them firmly wherever we go. They determine how we interpret an experience, whether we remember it as a good time or a bad time and whether we'd do it again or not. These barriers are the zones of comfort that we feel and they determine the basic core of what we are able to tolerate and endure.

In actuality, we can step beyond these boundaries into uncomfortable experiences that we are highly able to withstand and learn from. This is what we refer to as "stepping out of our comfort zone." From these experiences, we derive our meaning in life, and learn how to "learn" and adapt. By stepping out of our comfort zone, we develop critical thinking skills, self-esteem, and fortitude in coping with uncertain situations.

Our comfort zones are a complicated and interwoven tapestry of past memories with strands of mental, physical, emotional, social, and spiritual experiences running throughout. For some, comfort zones have wide and flexible boundaries. For others, they are seemingly carved from stone and planted solidly in a rigid and fixed position. Some people may be able to physically and mentally tolerate a hot climate without a shower and limited water and food for a prolonged period while many would find it difficult to endure and retreat to the comforts of an air-conditioned home immediately.

It is hard to know what a person's limits and range of tolerance are. Often, people don't know themselves, especially when placed in a new situation. If someone has never been camping or rafting it's almost impossible to know how they will react to mosquitoes, a lack of modern facilities for showering or being tossed into a swift and strong current in a fast flowing river. Thus, as an outdoor educator, it is important to know your participants before you challenge them in any of these areas.

The good news is that whatever a person's comfort zones are for any situation, with proper guidance they can expand the limits and boundaries of what they find pleasant and enjoyable.

Many students who are terrified of going outdoors and would never imagine catching a spider and identifying it, can be encouraged to do so. They may never even have had a direct experience with a 'terrifying' spider. Their fear of spiders may be the result of witnessing a parent, sibling or friends reaction to one. In this case, the arachnophobia might be socially determined without any direct experience. However, after a brief and fun introduction to being outdoors and the beauty and importance of eight legged creatures in the environment, they might completely change their view and attitude. The change is not always immediate or drastic but when a person is properly guided through an experience and allowed to expand their comfort zone they increase the limits of what they can tolerate.

Likewise students venturing into the forest at night may have misconceptions about what they think might happen (e.g., an animal jumping out of the dark and attacking them). They might even have a limited emotional comfort zone in relationship to being in the dark, especially if they have had a frightening past experience in a nighttime environment. But, as soon as they go outside in the dark and explore the nocturnal environment with a group and a good mentor, their comfort zone is expanded. They may report it as their favorite activity or memory and desire to re-experience the thrill of being outdoors at night.

As an outdoor education instructor, environmental education teacher, or adventure trip coordinator it is important to be aware that everyone has different levels of comfort for any activity you may facilitate.

In fact, many people can be highly inconsistent in their own comfort zones. For example, some students may be very comfortable with insects. They may enjoy watching and collecting specimens of almost any species. But, put a cockroach in their tent and they leap backwards screaming and yelping. On the other hand a student may be very tolerant of leeches but unable to deal

with heat or sun. Or a student may be extremely hearty and capable of tolerating anything you expose them to.

It is impossible to know where your students's comfort zones might be upon coming into a course, but you must be aware that each person has one. You need to be alert to their discomfort in various situations and adapt your lessons to accommodate them without slowing the learning occurring within the group. Therein lies the challenge!

Wetland Wisdom

"Does everyone have toilet paper? What about the first aid kit?"

"I hope we have enough reagents to run all of the nitrogen tests! What about the pH meter? Is it working?"

"I've got peanut butter and crackers!"

Doesn't sound like the typical research project, does it? But those are the words of an expedition leader during a last minute frenzy to make sure everything is in order for a trip into the Malaysian wilds.

For this outing, the destination would be the Tasek Bera wetland sanctuary. The trip promises the rare opportunity to be aided by the native people that call Tasek Bera home, the Orang Asli Semelai, and tap into their vast knowledge of the local ecosystem.

To many, science seems an esoteric discipline. The dreaded course requirements for university have sent many an undergraduate packing. Unfortunately, many scientists perpetuate the myth of an unobtainable storehouse of knowledge by disguising simple concepts in a whirlwind of specialized jargon. However, a hands-on experience in a beautiful location that emphasizes science may be just the key to exploding the myth that "science is hard".

To bring science alive, students set out on a three-day journey to answer basic questions about the ecology of Tasek Bera and demystify the process of scientific inquiry. All of this is accomplished while living in a long house and performing experiments in the great living laboratory of the Malaysian peat swamp environment! The students are not intimidated. Instead they are eager to go at it.

A multi-disciplinary team of instructors can demonstrate how various disciplines ranging from math, physics, biology and anthropology show students that everything truly is connected.

For this trip Mr. Roderick covers the math and physics, Mr. Miletti is the biologist, Mr. and Mrs. Daly take on geography, ethnobotany and anthropology while Mr. Peavy is the aquatic specialist.

A pre-trip discussion reveals that Mr. Roderick's group would be interested in measuring stream flow and use math and physics to answer their research questions.

Meanwhile, Mr. Miletti's group is keen to learn about the chemistry and biology of water quality. Yet another team wants to study the geographical and cultural aspects of the village around Tasek Bera.

Mrs. Daly, with her background in entomology and agriculture and an undeniable enthusiasm for ethno-botany, is invaluable.

Mr. Peavy lends a hand in the ichthyology, aquatic entomology and water quality departments.

Ms. Mohala from Wetlands International is also at hand to lend her knowledge and expertise of the Semalai, and act as translator from Bahasa Malaysia to English - an invaluable asset!

After a briefing on the bus ride down, the students begin to formulate research questions during the three-hour journey. Experiments in a controlled laboratory are what most students are used to, but Nature rarely fits our pre-conceived notions of how it works. That is why it's crucial to get outside and do science; that is also why field science almost never works out the way you think it's going to.

The multi-disciplinary approach taken in learning about Tasek Bera would prove invaluable in the days to come, as each student and teacher would have a different perspective and contribution to the overall success of the groups' endeavors.

Upon arrival at the jetty, we unload the gear and equipment from the bus into motor boats. The group is charged with excitement as the journey to the long house (our campsite) begins.

Barn swallows dash here and there as we glide over tannin stained water. Giant flame red dragonflies, with wings splayed, rest on emergent grasses. These are just a few of the amazing sites to be witnessed along the way. Suddenly, students realize a maze of Pandanu and Lepironia plants have replaced the tangle of sidewalks and concrete back home in Kuala Lumpur.

We settle into our longhouse and by nightfall research groups are established, each with a specific focus.

Mr. Peavy's group wants to investigate fish and insect populations and their distribution in several different stream habitats.

Mr. and Mrs. Daly's group focuses on forest soil chemistry and plant populations.

Mr. Roderick's group initial plan to investigate stream flow and water chemistry is revamped after a few initial experiments show that data obtained might be insufficient for reporting any differences. After some rethinking and discussion, the students decide to determine if there are any patterns in the distribution of Pandanu and Lepironia plants in relation to stream flow and the pH of the water.

Mr. Miletti's group decides they would like to know if there are any differences in water quality near the village as compared to the pristine wetland upstream.

A quick swim in the lake brings the day to an end and shortly, students and teachers are blissfully snoring in mosquito proof tents.

The next day turns out to be a gem. Shortly after breakfast the groups scatter to all corners of the wetland aided by their respective Orang Asli guide and research assistant. It seems clear skies and an early start, fueled by fried noodles, is all it takes to collect our data.

By mid-afternoon students return to base camp with their samples and bellies ready for a rice and chicken lunch. After a quick dip in the lake, the students head off again to collect more data.

The insect group stays back since they have collected all their samples. Instead, they jump into the arduous task of picking aquatic insects from the mud they have dredged up from the benthos.

By now Mr. Roderick's group has noticed a distinct pattern in the streamside vegetation distribution and is eager to document it and try and determine why these are located where they are.

Mr. and Mrs. Daly's group has collected samples near the long house, both in the forest and near the water's edge. By early afternoon they are taken to a similar site clear of human habitation to repeat sample collection.

Interestingly, this group learns there is little significant difference in the chemistry of soils gathered in the forest areas near and distant from human habitation. As a useful sideline, the students examine an inland Pandanus specifically used for building huts, and sample edible leaves and fruits pointed out to them by their guide, Mr Rahim. He also demonstrates how to make a drinking cup out of the leaf of one of the palm-like shrubs, showing that even the simplest conveniences can be provided by the forest!

That afternoon Mr. Daly's geography students interview Mr Hashim, manager of the Semelai's eco-tourism project, about the changes occurring among the Semelai with increasing modernization. He is very enthusiastic about eco-tourism, but emphatic that

the numbers of people visiting Tasek Bera must be kept low enough so as not to impact negatively on the environment that sustains his village.

Mr. Hashim envisages eco-tourism as economic and educational. Economic by providing income for the Semelai, and educational by nurturing respect for the environment and

culture of the Orang Asli Semelai among those people lucky enough to spend time at Tesak Bera.

A few hours later, everyone returns to camp. Immediately after a snack of fried bananas, they begin analyzing their samples and making sense of their field data.

On the way to an afternoon swim, the students notice several spectacular species of butterflies drinking near the water's edge. These are among the few groups of insects we see on the trip - surprising indeed what with all that forest around us. Perhaps this could provide the basis for a research question in the future.

Later in the evening the chief of the Orang Asli, Batin Hokin, joins us for a discussion about their marriage customs and the transition of the Semelai from a hunter-gatherer society to their recent venture into eco-tourism. We learn they only switched from their hunter-gatherer lifestyle in the 1980s and are growing more dependent on rice and rubber tapping for income and food. The chief says he is happy to see the eco-tourism working for them as it brings much needed income to the community while providing an education for both foreign and Malaysian students on the Semelai way of life.

Shortly thereafter everyone is ready for bed, but not before a few talented students treat the group to a little acoustic magic as they play and sing a few songs.

Once again, Mr. Roderick is serenaded by the sound of snores woven into a chorus of night frogs and insects.

The next morning the students write up their findings and compile all of their data. The teachers have never seen their students work as hard or more earnestly with such focus and determination.

A quick boat trip takes the students and their teachers back to the bus for the journey back to Kuala Lumpur. On the bus ride back they give mini-presentations which reflect their experiences and the research they performed. As we pull into the parking lot at school, students and teachers alike are both weary but wiser from the research and the trip.

The group is now part of the wetlands and it is part of them. The research conducted provides insights and knowledge into a place only a few are willing to investigate. This is truly an experience that cannot be captured within the confines of a classroom!

A Rice Barge Classroom

The soul of Siam resides where it always has, along the Chao Phraya – the "River of Kings." Traders and royal emissaries from all corners of the civilized world once navigated this fabled waterway to reach Ayutthaya, the "Venice of the East" and capital of Siam. The very word "Siam" many scholars believe, means "people of the river."

Today, a new generation of explorers sail this same route as part of the Magic Eyes Chao Phraya Barge Program – a floating classroom catering to Thai and international school students on one to five-day residential environmental education programs.

This project is the brainchild of Thai architect, Khun Mom Tri, who studied in the USA, and was strongly influenced by the Chewonki Foundation in Maine, a long-time leader in environmental education. Returning to Thailand with a new vision, he renovated an 80-year old, 20-meter teak rice barge, turning it into a floating laboratory for living and learning.

Mom Tri was concerned that Thai youth were losing their connections with the land, their culture and their identity. What type of future leaders would the Kingdom have if its youth knew only city streets and shopping malls? His plan was to literally immerse the students in their subject - to help them discover the Chao Phraya River, its environment, rich culture and fascinating history, so that they might one day become inspired and motivated to preserve and protect it. The program he envisioned was to stress hands-on investigation, critical thinking and cooperative problem solving.

The first trips began on the river in 1995 with participants from local schools, universities and Thai international schools. In 1997, Mom Tri turned the barge over to the Thai Environmental and Community Development Association, an NGO better known as Magic Eyes. Today, it's known as the Magic Eyes Chao Phraya Barge Program, and it has expanded its student base to include a stream of participants from foreign countries.

On a typical 3-day study cruise, students are welcomed aboard by the staff and immediately divided into work groups. No one is pampered on the barge, no matter how privileged their home life might be. While some youth swab the deck and empty soiled dishwater into the boat's treatment system, others prepare lunch, record weather and satellite positioning in the navigational log, or develop a group activity to be enjoyed by all before meal time.

Lynda Rolph, education manager aboard the barge, has the bubbly personality and patience of a primary school teacher, which she was in the UK before moving to teach in Thailand some years ago. Asked what she most enjoys about her job, she replies, "Just watching students see things for the first time - things like the first time in their lives they get mud on their shoes, or see a river crab or spider close up. I believe that this is the way children really learn. Never mind if it isn't math; they'll catch up with that later. Let the environment be the teacher."

Lynda loves her job in spite of the rigorous schedule. The barge currently serves over 30 schools and organizations, logging an average 264 trip days each year on the river.

Only at the height of the monsoon is the barge dry-docked for its costly annual maintenance. The staff are pretty well married to the barge; they have little time ashore for family and loved ones. Still, they demonstrate an exemplary passion for helping students open their eyes to the world around them.

Following lunch and clean-up, it's time to record observations as the barge slowly works its way up river. Students lie on the polished teak deck or prop themselves up with pillows as they examine the passing shoreline and answer questions from their study guide. "List 5 sources of pollution that are impacting the quality of the river ... 5 examples of solid waste garbage you see floating on the surface ... 5 species of wildlife ... 10 different economic activities." The list goes on.

A soothing breeze brings cool comfort to the students in their floating classroom. Thai music emanates from each passing temple to mingle with the delightful squeals and laughter of Thai children beating the midday heat by plunging from piers into the water. Rafts of water hyacinth float dreamily by in the Chao Phraya's slow but steady surge towards the sea. A few fish flip on the sur-

Back on board, it's time for a lively discussion on the sustainability of a community like Koh Kret, examining how environment, economy and society each affect land-use development. The lesson continues a few hours later, as they stop to visit the Pathum Thani market. The students must do their own shopping for the food they'll cook over the next few days, so there's a briefing session before going ashore. Should they accept plastic bags from the vendors with every purchase? When the students learn that

face, and a Brahminy kite swoops down to snatch one. The students take it all in, subliminally, along with their lesson.

It's mid-afternoon when the barge pulls ashore at Koh Kret, an island in the river settled by Mon refugees from Burma in the 1700s. The students receive a history briefing before they go ashore to see for themselves how this thriving pottery-producing community derives its living from the river clay and river life. They buy drinks in reusable clay pots and enjoy local snacks of tempura shrimp, river greens and flowers served in bio-degradable, beautifully crafted banana leaf.

more than 500,000 tons of plastic and Styrofoam are discarded in Thailand every year, they opt for reusable cloth bags. There is no preparation for the culture shock, however. "I really hated the market," says one girl. "Watching all the frogs and fish and eels squirming around was really disgusting. Even though I don't like it, I know I'm here to see new things, so I guess I just have to get over being sick."

The group spends their first night tied up to a small pier in a natural setting, an ideal situation for early-morning

bird study. A dawn stroll through the nearby wetlands turns up 11 species of birds, from the huge Asian open-billed storks flying high overhead to a dazzling pair of Blue-tailed bee eaters.

As the barge continues its voyage the study focus shifts to monitoring water quality. Students are divided into teams to perform nine water-quality tests. These range from simple exercises to record temperature, turbidity and pH, to more complex analyses such as determining nitrate and phosphate levels, fecal coliform bacteria, dissolved oxygen,

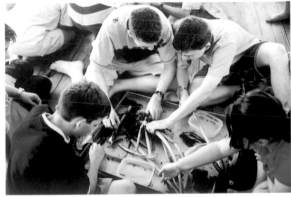

total dissolved solids, and biochemical oxygen demand. Chemistry, physics, biology and math all come into play as the data is combined to get a water quality index for this portion of the river.

Having determined the water quality stands at 64.71 (mid-range pollution), most of the students slip into lifejackets and plunge overboard for a swim. "I was surprised how polluted the water actually is when we did the testing," says a 15-year old boy. "But I jumped in anyway. I was so hot."

Following the swim and lunch, everyone turns their attention to water hyacinths. Combining geography, history, anthropology and biology, students learn that this freshwater aquatic plant, which is a native to Brazil, was brought to Java by Portuguese traders and then transferred to Thailand by King Rama V because he thought the mauve blossoms would look lovely in the royal gardens. The exotic species has now invaded most Thai waterways.

Dissecting the hyacinth root system in large metal trays set out on deck totally captivates the students. They're amazed to find so many tiny invertebrates hidden in the plant's hair-like roots, from crabs and freshwater shrimp to snails,

leeches and the nymph stages of flies. "I'm glad we went for our swim before we did this exercise," says one squeamish student of her discoveries.

There's never a dull moment on the barge. When the participants aren't engaged in study, work groups, or team-building games, they might be exploring a canal by canoe, or playing games with Thai children in the schoolyard of a riverside village.

On the second night of the trip, the barge ties up beside the pier of Wat Niwet, a Buddhist temple built by King Rama V. The students are given cultural background regarding Theravada Buddhism and instructed on the etiquette of alms-giving. At 5 am everyone is awakened from a deep sleep in the communal quarters below deck to help prepare food and flower offerings for the monks. Standing barefoot in the first light of day, international students offer steamed rice, milk, fruit and flowers to Thai novice monks their same age. Later that day, the group finds itself in the ancient ruins of Ayutthaya. Following a thorough historic briefing on this 417-year center of Thai civilization, it's time to explore the site with senses wide open.

Lynda Rolph is a master of creative visualization. Amid the ruins of Wat Pra Sri Sampet,

under the cool shade of acacia trees, she instructs the students to lie on their backs, close their eyes and listen. Through guided imagery she transports them back in time to 1776 - imagining they are Portuguese traders arriving from a long voyage on the very day the Burmese sacked the city. Every detail is visualized through imagery, sight, sound, taste, texture and smell - the red dust rising from the foot path, the thunder of war drums and elephants marching in the distance, the aroma of fish grilling on charcoal, the smooth, powdery texture of the white palace wall as they run their fingers along it.

Following the exercise, students are challenged to write their impressions of that day from different perspectives. One girl writes from the viewpoint of an invading Burmese elephant; another boy describes the soul-searching of a reluctant Burmese warrior.

These youth are seeing history with fresh, magical eyes through a 3-day experience they will never forget. One can only hope that more students might one day be offered similar immersion experiences in a range of geographical and historical locations. There's more than enough magic in the world - if we only have eyes to see.

Malaysia Week

What are you most afraid of?
"Leeches!"
"Using the toilet outside!"
"Tigers eating me!"

What are you most looking forward to?
"Camping in a tent, I've never done that before."
"Swimming in the river! What's that like?"
"Eating the camp food! I hope it's good!"

When asked these questions prior to embarking on our five-day foray into the Malaysian wilderness, these were some of the responses students gave.

The International School of Kuala Lumpur (ISKL) in Malaysia is extremely fortunate to have a 'week without walls' built into the curriculum. Every March the Middle School closes its doors for five days. The white boards stand empty and the classrooms echo with silence while the students, teachers and administrators set out to various outdoor adventure locales spread throughout Peninsular Malaysia.

With 18 locations to choose from there is no shortage of adventure to be had. Various challenges await students, ranging from white water rafting, jungle trekking, boating, coral reef snorkeling, and climbing Gunung

Tahan, the highest mountain on the peninsula at 2,187 meters. Students make their choices based on their preference for beach, mountain, lake, river or rainforest, and/or the levels of challenge - ranging from moderate to very challenging - at the respective sites.

Malaysia Week is probably the most anticipated event of the year and the day itineraries are posted is probably the single most exciting day in Middle School! Students crowd around to see if they have been assigned to the location of their first choice. Some literally run up and down the hallways squealing and shouting, "I'm going to Sibu Island!"; "I'm going to Belum rainforest!" or "I'm going to the Perak River!"

One of the most coveted sites is Endau Rompin National Park. Endau Rompin contains some of the oldest rainforest on the planet, estimated to be 160-200 million years old. The park is also a refuge for endangered species such as the Asian elephant, the Sumatran rhino and tigers. An endemic fan palm (Livistona endauensis) was only recently discovered, named and described. Obviously, a visit to this incredible location allows students to experience things that simply cannot be accomplished in the confines of the classroom.

The atmosphere is electric with excitement as the bus is unloaded at the park headquarters. All of the students' questions will soon be answered.

Their first adventure is a boat ride upriver and then a trek to the camp that will be home for the next few days. Students are taught how to set up tents, a task that few have experience in. After setting up they familiarize themselves with their surroundings by completing a scavenger hunt and locating common forest plants.

Many of the students have rarely been so close to Nature. Living in their condominiums and sterile environs they have never had an opportunity to dig in the dirt and get up close and personal with the flora of Malaysia. A brief introductory activity lets them know it's more than "OK" to get down and dirty, allowing them to overcome a bit of anxiety through a comfortable and fun activity.

By late afternoon, a meal of noodles and a swim in the cool river are in order. Swimming in a natural body of water is something few urbanite students rarely get to do, if ever! A little nervous about the river, some of the students wait for the guides and instructors to take a dip before they jump in! It's intriguing and telling that they are afraid of a swimming hole because it isn't square, blue and full of chlorine! Soon their inhibitions disappear and the water games begin. Not many activities have such a universal appeal. Swimming in a clean and clear river with Racquet-tailed Drongos singing in the canopy is a treat most unusual yet special for these students.

The night activity reveals nocturnal critters and fluorescent fungi. Again the students are full of nervous energy and visions of tigers jumping out of the bush before the exploration begins. As soon as they hit the trail their fears subside. The

intense sound of cicadas singing and the mysterious glow-in-the-dark fungi help them forget their fears. A short time later they return to camp giddy with stories of how they had survived the jungle at night.

Weary from the day's events, the camp falls silent early in the evening under a gibbous moon shining high in the sky.

During the course of the next few days, the forest neophytes slowly become familiar and comfortable with the natural world.

Stick insects, carnivorous pitcher plants, elephant dung, cicadas, preying mantis and leeches become a real and tangible part of their daily world, if only for a short while. What was once an abstract concept found only in textbooks or on TV is now something they have smelled, touched, tasted and heard.

The telling tale of their shift in attitude occurs during the final night when they study invertebrates illuminated by torch light. Students

who were previously frightened by the mere thought of a beetle or spider and would never venture out into the forest at night are now expertly sampling nocturnal insects and sketching them in their journals. Their confidence and excitement is clearly evident as they discover first hand the critters they have been hearing at camp. In some instances, they have to be reminded to slow down and take their time!

The transformation is incredible. The students leaving Endau Rompin are certainly not the same students that had arrived a few days earlier. Rafting, boating, swimming, plant studies, jungle trekking and insect hunts has metamorphosed these citified students into budding naturalists.

The value of spending a few days outside close to Nature and learning in its living laboratory cannot be overstated. Getting outdoors and escaping the confines of the classroom has given these students skills, experiences and memories they are not likely to forget. Instead of simply reading about the rainforest and its incredible diversity of flora and fauna, these students have learned how to read the forest itself, breathe its intoxicating perfumes and interpret the incredible stories it tells!

Reefs to Rainforests

The night sounds of the rainforest gradually fade away as the first longing calls of male gibbon, crying for mates, signal the dawn. Some of the 24 international school students, that have spent their first jungle night ever sleeping in two-person floating raft houses, are awoken by the gibbon songs; others need a little more encouragement.

"Time to get up, everyone!" a Thai staff member cheerily announces as he walks the long, wobbly walkway connecting the floating huts. "Dawn Safari starts in 20 minutes!"

The eastern sky is already ablaze in color when the first, gung-ho youth emerge from their huts at 6:00 am and plunge head first into the lake for a quick morning dip. Others squat at the edge of the bamboo walkway and gently wash the sleep from their eyes with their hands, all the while absorbing through every pore the magic of the morning. Everyone needs to wake up to the fact that there's no maid service here, or chauffeurs to drive them off to school. This isn't Kansas anymore, Dorothy.

Three long-tail boats break the silence as they work their way to dockside to transport the students in different directions across

Cheow Lan Lake - a vast reservoir that lies at the heart of southern Thailand's Khoa Sok National Park. Armed with binoculars, topographical maps, and bird and mammal identification guides, three student teams board their boats and start exploring the shoreline for signs of animal life. They will spend these hours of first light, when diurnal species are most active, to inventory gibbon families, langur troops, and carefully plot the locations of hornbill nesting sites. They are taking part in the first such inventories ever conducted here, survey information that is crucial for the park in determining impacts on wildlife populations from poaching.

Two hours later, back at the floating raft houses, everyone discusses their sightings over a hearty breakfast of mango pancakes, fresh tropical fruit and hearty bowls of 'kow tum' - Thai rice and pork soup. Once all the sightings are plotted on the maps, student teams hold break-out sessions with their Thai guide during which each individual has an opportunity to commit to becoming a hornbill, langur, flying fox or gibbon 'guardian' for life.

Through their studies and first hand observations, each student now fully understands the role 'keystone' species play in Nature. Those that so choose can now make a pledge to the group that they will do everything possible, from educating others to making personal changes in their own behavior, to help protect the species they adopted. Beautifully embroidered patches, depicting a hornbill, gibbon, langur or giant fruit bat are then awarded to each 'guardian' to be proudly worn on their jackets or caps.

It's been a full morning, but the day has just begun. Following breakfast and a few hours to swim and kayak in the lake, a picnic lunch is prepared and the students set off on their next adventure – a 3 hour interpretive hike through a rainforest and an Indiana Jones-style adventure studying cave ecology while passing through a 500-meter cave passage. An hour later, emerging from the darkness after exploring bat chambers with giant cave spiders, negotiating underground waterfalls, and swimming through a cold cave creek to the exit, the students' eyes are as wide as elephant tracks.

"Wow!" one student exclaims, as he 'high-fives' his classmates, "I never thought our school would ever allow us to do something as awesome and wild as this! Can we go through the cave again?"

Reefs to Rainforests is an 8-day environmental education, immersion program that has been operating in the south of Thailand for nearly a decade. Combining fun and soft adventure, it explores seven Southeast Asian ecosystems: tropical evergreen forest, rainforest, karsts and caves, fresh water wetlands, mangroves, coral reefs and inter-tidal zones. The program, operated by Thai Nature Education, is attended by a growing number of international schools either as part of a "week without walls" program, or during school holiday periods. The educational value of the experience is such that several

American universities offer course credits to teachers that take part in special sessions.

Reefs to Rainforests is a good example of how an extended school outing can combine all three elements of effective environmental learning: 1) it expands environmental awareness, 2) it allows for intimate moments in Nature that deepen a sense of belonging, and 3) it provides opportunities for Earth stewardship.

A lot of information comes at the students pretty fast during the program, but because they are learning with all their senses wide open, the retention level is much higher than in a classroom setting. Participants are never pressured with homework or formal exams; instead the learning is presented as play. Each student is given a small, pocket-sized text book: *Reefs to Rainforests / Mangroves to Mountains - A guide to South Thailand's Natural Wonders,* that can be used as a reference guide. Fun quizzes are presented from time to time by way of reviewing the material. For instance, every student that wants to receive a beautiful batik program t-shirt, or a colorful *tangkae* (Thai fisherman pants), must first be able to answer a question about the ecosystems they have been studying. A similar game might be played to receive extra dessert at meal time.

Even more important than the information presented, *Reefs to Rainforests* offers quiet moments for a student's personal introspection. Floating quietly under a firmament of stars on a 'Night Safari' is a profound experience for most urban youth. Simple events like watching the sun rise over a mountain range, experiencing a tropical rain squall sweeping across the lake, being lulled to sleep by the night orches-

tration of frogs from the cozy comfort of a hammock, or exploring tide pools of brilliant starfish while the sun sets over a tidal flat... all provide intimate, and often profound, moments with Nature.

The third key component of environmental education is stewardship, allowing youngsters the opportunity to realize that Nature - given half a chance - can be as resilient as youth themselves.

Students on Thailand's *Reefs to Rainforest* program engage in stewardship activities in several ways: through the wildlife surveys and mapping project at Khao Sok National Park, and by replanting mangrove trees in a degraded area adjacent to a UNESCO Bio-

sphere Reserve in Ranong. Sore muscles and chaffed hands, from a few hours of planting 250 mangrove seedlings, is a small price to pay for the pride these students will have when they can one day show their own children a mature forest they helped to restore.

South Thailand is an astonishingly diverse region of the world, displaying many distinct ecosystems in relative close proximity to one another. In addition to the two days spent at Khao Sok National Park experiencing tropical evergreen forests, students also hike through a remnant patch of lowland rainforest in Krabi Province – part of the oldest terrestrial ecosystem on Earth.

At Thale Noi, on the Gulf of Thailand's side of the Thai/Malay Peninsula, students travel by boat through a Ramsar Site – a wetland of global significance – where more species of waterfowl reside on a single lake than can be found in most countries in Europe. The Andaman Sea side of the peninsula, by contrast, offers some of the world's best dive sites on Koh Surin and the offshore islands of Trang Province. Here students, often for the first time, peer below the surface at the richest ecosystem on Earth - the dazzling coral reefs.

Later that evening, as the sea recedes across broad tidal flats, they have an opportunity to view tide pools, the ecosystem where science believes life itself began.

Lessons in mangrove ecology are not presented from text books in stuffy classrooms, but by paddling through the mangroves in two-person kayaks. It is not every day students get to see monkeys that eat crabs, fish that climb trees, and seeds that germinate before leaving their parent tree.

One of the most popular experiences of all is doing a macro-invertebrate study of a stream. Armed with dip nets, magnifying lenses, note books and charts (illustrating a great range of macro-invertebrate species), the students set out on their aquatic hunts. Wading through a shallow, fast flowing

creek, they carefully overturn rocks and search under cut banks with their nets for their mini prey. The type of aquatic insects present, they soon learn, determines the health of a watershed.

"One of the most wonderful things about Reefs to Rainforests," says ISB teacher Anne Hayden-Gilbert, "is the opportunity for students to learn in a cooperative rather than competitive environment." With so much emphasis on competition in school for grades, sports, scholarships, boyfriends/ girlfriends - outdoor education can offer youth a pleasant reprieve from intense social pressures.

Lending a helping hand to someone scared and struggling along the course of the cave hike, sharing personal feelings while sitting in a group circle around a candle or campfire, or working together as a team to construct a shelter, build a fire and forage wild foods in a simulated survivor session - are all experiences that foster cooperative rather than competitive spirits.

Reefs to Rainforests is a concept that is easily adaptable to other locations in the world. A Grizzlies & Glaciers environmental adventure program in northern British Columbia, Canada now combines fun and soft adventure in the study of seven ecosystems: old growth temperate rainforests, salmon streams, fresh water lakes, alpine and sub-alpine forests, glaciers and Pacific marine and tidal ecosystems. In addition to the great learning potential, participants enjoy white water rafting, forest and alpine treks, grizzly bear viewing and whale watching.

Similar programs could be offered almost anywhere there is a rich diversity of environments to serve as outdoor classrooms. The important lessons for students studying these systems is to realize the fuzzy boundaries between them. There are no hard, inflexible lines in Nature; living things in one ecosystem often interact with, and depend upon, living things in adjacent ecosystems. Learning the complexity of these interactions, and the ways in which human activities both depend upon them and impact upon them, is the most important lesson of all.

Rediscovery

Yellow eyes emerge eerily from the darkness and stare back at a 15-year old native boy across the fading flicker of his solo fire. He has been alone in the wilderness of northern Canada for more than fifteen hours and he's wondering if his own eyes are starting to play tricks on him.

When a female wolf emerges slowly into the full light of the small fire, the boy does not panic but whispers to himself, "Stay calm; stay calm." Native elders back at base camp, who helped prepare him for this rite of passage, had told him that his spirit guardian might come to him in an animal form, possibly in a dream. The boy finds the courage not to flinch as the tawny colored canine cautiously approaches to sniff him. Though both hearts are racing, neither the boy nor the beast displays any visible signs of aggression or fear.

As the fire dies down to embers, and the night turns cold, the she wolf curls up to sleep beside the boy and keeps him warm, as if he were her long lost pup. When the young man awakens at dawn, she is gone.

The tale of this extraordinary solo adventure, when told to other participants back at base camp, is met with incredulity and a good deal of razzing. "Yeah right; as if!" the kids tease him. "What kind of berries were you on, man?"

"Hey, wait a minute," one of the campers interrupts those deriding the story teller. "Look, he's got wolf hair all over his jacket!"

Encounters such as this are rare indeed, but even less profound moments for a person voluntarily spending 24-hours alone in the wilderness, can prove transformational. The *Rediscovery* program knows this well and has been providing opportunities for youth to have intimate, self-discovery experiences in Nature for the past three decades in more than forty different wilderness camp settings.

Rediscovery began in 1978 on the remote shores of Haida Gwaii (the Queen Charlotte Islands) - an archipelago of 150 islands on the Pacific coast of British Columbia near the Alaska border. It came about as a community response to kids in crisis, and as a means of revitalizing Haida culture with a generation of indigenous youth that were rapidly losing their links with the land, their customs and traditions. Right from the start, *Rediscovery* was integrated. It drew together Haida and non-native peoples as never be-

fore, stressing cross-cultural respect at every level from community supporters to board members, camp staff to participants.

Rediscovery was founded on a simple but all encompassing philosophy. It's mission statement said it all: "Drawing on the strength of native traditions and the wisdom of elders, and with a spirit of love and reverence for the land, *Rediscovery* strives to help youth of all ages discover the world within themselves, the cultural worlds between them, and the natural world around them."

Looking within to find strength youngsters never knew they had seemed an obvious place to start as many of the participants drawn to the program were victims of family violence, broken homes and various types of abuse. Providing an alcohol, drug-free and safe setting, strong peer role models, and experienced counselors was part of the reason for *Rediscovery's* success. But much more can be attributed to the healing powers of Nature itself. The first *Rediscovery* camp (still in operation) was located forty air miles from the nearest town, road or telephone. The isolation was chosen deliberately to fully remove participants from the negative influences of town, and to provide better opportunities for food gathering and wilderness adventure. Just as importantly, the isolation served to create a social microcosm, a small but cohesive group that needed to get along with one another in order to survive.

The format worked beyond all expectations, and is still in use today. Teenagers take part in 2-week sessions, while pre-teen programs are shortened to 10 days. This seems to be the optimum time period for urban youth to get the greatest value from a wilderness experience without getting 'bushed'.

The schedule for the first five days in base camp is the same for both teen and pre-teen groups. Everyone gets up early, joins in group stretches and a run along a beautiful expanse of sandy beach before breakfast. Camp chores are also shared responsibilities. Following breakfast and dinner, work groups rotate between washing dishes, splitting firewood, fetching water, and cleaning up base camp facilities and grounds.

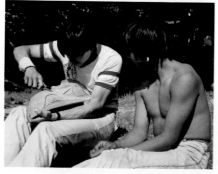

Participants are never asked to take on a chore that the staff themselves won't willingly join them in. *Rediscovery* strives to create a healthy family environment - not a boot camp.

Workshops and day outings also operate on a rotational basis. One group of 6-8 campers might set off after breakfast with a picnic lunch on a full day outing to learn about Haida heritage at several nearby abandoned village sites that still contain petroglyphs, stone forts, remnants of longhouses and totem poles. During this time they may gather cedar bark for making baskets, or harvest shellfish and octopus from the same tidal flats the former villagers relied upon for thousands of years. *Rediscovery* participants might even use costumes to act out a scene from centuries past - a wedding arrangement to cement ties between two villages, a shamanistic healing ceremony, or a gift-giving feast to honor a new chief.

Another group might be taking kayaking lessons and learning traditional crafts from the elders back at base camp. Still another team might be learning about forest, bog and inter-tidal ecology through a variety of experiential exercises designed to tune in all of their senses and help them better understand the wonderful complexity of Nature. (Many of the activities presented in this book were first developed by the author when he was Program Director the first seven years on Haida Gwaii Rediscovery).

In the late afternoon, when all the groups return to base camp, there is time to relax, catch up on journals, or enjoy group sports before dinner. An incentive that helps to speed up evening chores is to join in the fun of playing *Rediscovery* and native games on the beach until sunset. It is then time for *Spirit Spot*.

Sunset is the most reflective time of the day; even wars have been known to observe cease fires for this introspective moment. Every participant on *Rediscovery* uses this 30-40 minute time period to enjoy solitude at their own private *Spirit Spot*. A *Spirit Spot* is nothing more than a place in Nature that suits the mood of, and is reserved for the exclusive use of, the participant that chooses it. It needn't be far away from base camp, but from the location each youngster chooses they should not look out upon any camp facilities or another person. By returning to this same location, day after day and at the same time, animals become accustomed to a non-threatening, regular human presence. Birds will start landing on branches nearby, deer will forage closer and closer, a mouse or squirrel might become bold enough to nibble a participant's fruit snack..

Spirit Spot is a quiet time for the whole camp, and for many participants it becomes one of their most enduring memories of camp. Sometimes a child, not wanting to return to a dysfunctional home environment, will run away and hide on the day of departure from camp. These youngsters can invariably be found at their *Spirit Spots*.

Quiet, reflective moments in Nature have become so rare in today's hectic urban lifestyles that some Rediscovery programs take kids through a creative visualization exercise before they leave camp otherwise known as 'Portable Spirit Spot'. This exercise allows each child to return in their mind to the peaceful state of their *Spirit Spot* any time throughout their lives. The evening *Spirit Spot* also helps prepare youngsters for their 24-hour *Solo/Vision Quest* by expanding their comfort zone being alone in Nature.

Most *Rediscovery* camps of two-week duration or longer have a 3-5 day expedition component. This not only prevents any monotony from developing in base camp life, but it teaches a whole new set of skills, improves fitness levels, and provides an even greater opportunity for group bonding. *Rediscovery* expeditions can take many forms from an extended coastal hike or sea kayak adventure, to mountain climbing and river running. The first *Rediscovery* camp on Haida Gwaii, for instance, does a 5-day hiking expedition down the west coast of Graham Island. Along the way there are endless opportunities for personal growth and discovery. The hikers learn about the geology of the region by finding ammonites in the shale outcrops along shore. They spend a night like cave men, sleeping in a huge cave carved by the sea into an ancient volcanic plug. They gather mussels, pick berries and

wild teas, fish for trout, and thrill to count-less wildlife encounters - the flight of a per-egrine falcon, seals bobbing in the kelp beds, an orca spouting offshore, eagles feeding on a dead sea lion, a family of otters running into the forest, a black bear scavenging the shoreline, or the courtship ritual of sand hill cranes. Every moment on the expedition is one of deep immersion.

When the campers return to base camp, the location and facilities that once seemed re-mote and primitive, now feel like coming home. There's a camp cook to help prepare meals, the luxury of outhouses, beds and lots of grub. A celebratory mood sweeps the camp and there might even be an evening dance to rejoice in the group's accomplish-ment.

The day following the end of the expedition is set aside for the most important *Redis-covery* experience of all - the *Solo/Vision Quest*. For many thousands of years 'vision quests' were the traditional rite of passage for many indigenous tribes of North America. A young person coming into adulthood would spend a period of days, weeks or even months alone in the wilderness, praying and fasting for a vision that would guide them in their adult life. An animal might appear in a real or dream state that would become that person's 'spirit guardian' for life. Many an-cient pictographs and petroglyphs are be-lieved to mark sacred sites used for vision quests.

The *Rediscovery* solo experience is a very condensed version of this time-honored tra-dition. Unlike some wilderness adventure programs with para-military origins that have compulsory three day solos as part of a boot camp-style regimen, *Rediscovery* solos are always voluntary. Any participant that feels the time is right in their life to accept this challenge is encouraged to do so, but no one is made to feel less for preferring to stay in camp.

A special solo ceremony takes place in base camp before participants are led out to their solo sites by their guides. A vigil fire is lit during the ceremony and it is tended by those remaining in camp until every soloist safely returns. Solo participants are allowed to take

with them a raw potato, fresh water, a sleeping bag, 2-3 matches, warm clothing, rain gear and an emergency whistle. During their time alone they may construct a shel-ter, build a small fire in a safe location, and forage for any wild foods they can abso-lutely identify as edible. An unobtrusive spot check is made of each soloist by the staff just before dark, and all solo sites are care-fully recorded on a map for safety. To safe-guard against bear encounters, soloists are not allowed to take scented soaps, perfume, cologne, toothpaste, or any food other than their raw potato.

It is hard to fully explain the power of this experience for young people, but there may be no greater event in their lives that puts them in such intimate touch with the forces of Nature and their own true nature. Very often, the biggest, strongest bully in camp is unable to complete a solo experience; in-deed most are reluctant to even attempt it. Asked to explain the apparent paradox, the native elders put it simply: "The reason that person behaves that way is because they don't know themselves, they don't like them-selves; no one wants to spend 24 hours alone with someone they don't know or like."

Yet another ceremony welcomes the solo-ists back to camp on the last day of the pro-gram, and this is the biggest celebration of

all. All day long a huge feast of wild foods is prepared by everyone in camp; when the participants aren't cooking they are working on dance masks and costumes for the closing ceremony. Each hike group is responsible with their leaders to put on a performance around the closing council fire that retells one of the Haida legends they learned, or their own epic story from a shared experience during the expedition. Ceremony night is a very important part of the Rediscovery experience. It is a time to acknowledge each camper for their personal achievements and to celebrate the completion of a remarkable trip together.

Haida Gwaii Rediscovery never envisioned itself becoming a model program that would inspire similar camps throughout the world, but today there are more than forty community-based *Rediscovery* camps operating in Canada, the United States, Thailand, Nepal, Ghana, Dominica, the United Kingdom, Austria, Sweden and Germany. Each camp is independently administered and creates a program that reflects the uniqueness of the location and indigenous culture it is based upon.

The Rediscovery International Foundation (RIF) was set up in 1985 to serve as an

umbrella support organization. It helps keep the family of camps connected through newsletters, conferences, and an annual leadership training program at United World College in Canada that helps *Rediscovery* camps live up to the very high health and safety standards they have set for themselves.

Increasingly, RIF is acting to facilitate 'quests' that bring together many *Rediscovery* communities, and youth from throughout the world, to share the joys of engaging in major expeditions. Canoe Quest 2003 - 'Retracing the Ancestral Highway' saw all four First Nations living along the Skeena River in northern British Columbia come together with 12 international youth in a historic paddle from Kispiox to the Pacific. An even larger expedition in 2006 will bring together coastal and interior communities in a paddle from Kitimat to Bella Coola titled 'Salmon Nations Pulling Together'.

In the final analysis, *Rediscovery* measures its success not in the number of camps it has inspired, but in the number of youth that have had transformational experiences at them. Viewing the wilderness as a homeland, rather than a frontier to be conquered, was one of the guiding principals set down by native elders at the very outset. It is the goal of *Rediscovery* camps everywhere to

bring children to that wonderful place where they see Nature as their home, and care deeply for the place they inhabit.

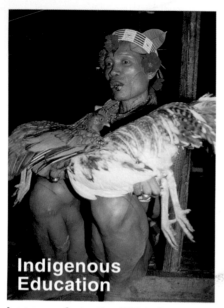

Indigenous Education

Lessons from the Illiterate

Five Mentawai shamen, clad in loin cloths, ring tiny bells and sing a slow repetitive chant in high and low octaves as they enter a hypnotic trance deep in the jungles of Siberut Island, Indonesia. The large clan house where they have gathered is packed with relatives that have come to take part in a ceremonial pig feast. What makes this event different from countless other feasts the Mentawai have conducted down through the millennia is the fact that 15 international students from one of Asia's most prestigious schools are among the guests. They are taking part in a 12-day immersion program that has brought them to one of the most isolated places on Earth to learn from of Southeast Asia's most archaic tribes.

As the students arrive and the ceremony begins, a Sikeri – a Mentawai shaman – carries a chicken around the large open-air room, gently brushing it against all those present. "Bring no harm to those living here, or those gathered here," he intones the bird's spirit. "Tell your relatives that you have always been well cared for, and know that you have many kin to survive you in this world. We will forever honor you with your feathers placed in this uma."

Without a squawk or flutter of wings in protest, the chicken's neck is slowly extended and tweaked. A few wing and tail feathers are placed in the roof thatching before the bird is cut open to divine the future. Several Sikeri gather to interpret the message contained in the pattern of veins and arteries surrounding the transparent membrane of the bird's intestines. All the omens are good.

Never having seen a chicken outside a Styrofoam tray in the sanitized setting of a supermarket, some of the students have difficulty with what they are witnessing, but there is more to come. A pig now squeals its death cry as it is hauled to the entrance of the 'uma' (the clan house) where it is stabbed in the jugular with a magically appointed dagger. Once all the blood has drained into a bowl for the feast, two strong boys haul the carcass to the edge of the jungle to singe off the hair by fire before the carcass is butchered. The students are aghast, but also in wonder as the pig is cooked and cut up into equal portions for

every man, woman, child and infant present in the 'uma'.

"Why does an infant, still nursing from its mother, get the same portion of meat as the headman of the clan?" they ask their interpreter. The Mentawai guide cannot imagine where such a question comes from. Finally in exasperation, he replies, "Can you not see? Only the infant's body is small; the spirit is already large."

In time the international school students will come to realize that the Mentawai are not only an incredibly egalitarian society, but they revere children perhaps more than any other people. The Mentawai never punish or speak harshly to their children for fear it will drive the spirit from the child's body and bring on sickness or death. The Mentawai, in fact, have no words in their language for the plethora of social ills that face youth in modern cultures: stress, alcohol and drug dependency, physical, emotional and sexual abuse, teen depression and suicide. Mentawai children spend their time in the constant company of one or both parents, who themselves enjoy more leisure time than almost any other society. Some of the

international school students, by contrast, are the sons and daughters of CEOs, heads of state, and diplomatic corps parents whose demands of the work place allow them a mere 17 minutes each day with their children.

Through small, incremental moments like this the students come to realize that Mentawai culture may not be as primitive as it first appeared. They start to see a highly advanced social order with sophisticated methods employed to avoid conflict and right wrongs – a democratic, age and gender egalitarian society they never imagined possible. Though the Mentawai have no written language and carry no letters after their names, they are now acting as educators to some of the most privileged students in Asia.

"Now I know the true meaning of education," a student wrote in her school newspaper when she returned from Siberut. "It's to be led by two 6-year olds flawlessly through the forest, and to be taught what I can eat along the way."

There are an estimated 300 million indigenous peoples in the world today, with over half of them living in Asia. Many of these people have no written language, but retain rich oral traditions dating back to the beginning of human time. Their stories, passed on from generation to generation, are tens of thousands of years older than the oldest books. And yet, modern societies in the name of education are on the verge of eliminating this treasure trove of knowledge through compulsory elementary education.

Equating illiteracy with ignorance, the United Nations has set a goal of ending illiteracy worldwide. While the goal may seem legitimate, even noble in literate societies, it is dangerously misdirected when applied to oral tradition societies. Without indigenous educators teaching their own traditional knowledge in their own setting and in their own language, oral tradition societies will be obliterated. An instant generation gap will be created between children and their parents if they are forced to learn a completely new set of values taught to them in a foreign language their parents do not understand.

To help bring about the paradigm shift that will be necessary for the world community to more fully recognize the rights of indigenous peoples and the wealth of knowledge they hold – information that could prove vital to human survival – several innovative learning opportunities have begun. The Mentawai of Indonesia and the Moken of Thailand's Andaman Sea have both agreed to be teachers to visiting international schools. Neither of these societies is being exposed to outsiders for the first time, nor are they being sequestered as living museums of humanity's Neolithic past. They are instead acting as willing partners in an experiment in education that may prove crucial to their very survival. If Asia's most prestigious schools can recognize the inherent values in Mentawai and Moken cultures perhaps there will be less government pressures to eliminate their knowledge base by forcing modern ways upon them.

Establishing the level of rapport and trust to bring about this opportunity for education

did not come about overnight. Co-author Thom Henley spent twelve years learning from the Mentawai on Siberut Island. Long before the first school groups arrived, he wrote a book on their culture *(Living Legend of the Mentawai)* and deferred all revenues from sales to Mentawai health and education projects. In spite of their isolation, the Mentawai have had visitors coming to their villages for many years – mostly budget back-packers in search of a blank place on the map – so the arrival of student groups was not seen as an intrusion. The Mentawai themselves encourage the school visits for the revenue it brings and because they absolutely adore children.

It was a very different association that opened the door to educational possibilities with the Moken (Sea Gypsies) living on Koh Surin, Thailand. Thanks to their oral traditions that teach their children the dangers of a rapidly receding sea level, none of the 200 Moken on Surin Island died in the 26 December tsunami that claimed nearly half a million lives in South Asia in 2004. Still they lost all of their boats, their homes, tools and food provisions. It was through the author's tsunami relief efforts with the Moken that the door opened to the possibility of a "Moken Immersion" school.

More than 50 Moken men are hired by Koh Surin National Park to be boatmen for tourists in the high season (November-April) when the park is open to the public. The tsunami destroyed this opportunity for cash to help supplement the Moken's subsidence, seafaring lifestyles, so they were grateful for any type of employment that might help to replace this. Normally looked down upon as second class Thai citizens, and not even paid the minimum wage by the National Park, the Moken were amazed to see Thai and foreign students respectfully greeting them as their teachers.

Both the Moken and the Mentawai live on isolated islands, the principal factor that has allowed them to retain their time-honored traditions. But the educational experience each tribe offers – like the cultures themselves – are really quite different.

Mentawai Magic

A trip to the Mentawai Islands is a magical adventure; it is about as far off the beaten path as one is likely to get. Jakarta International School was the first to send student groups to Siberut in 2003 as part of Grade 9 Project Week. United Nations International School Hanoi, was quick to follow in 2006. Today there is a growing interest in this approach to education by more and more schools.

The port of Padang in Western Sumatra is the jump off point for students bound for Siberut (the largest of the Mentawai isles), as there are no airstrips on the islands as yet. During the 8-10 hour ferry crossing of the Mentawai Strait, students learn of the incredible depth of this oceanic trench and the role it has played in separating the Mentawai Islands from the rest of Southeast Asia for the past million years. This isolation has resulted in the highest endemism in Southeast Asia, and the highest level of endemic primates found anywhere in the world. It is not without reason, the students learn, that these islands are called 'Asia's Galapagos'.

Arriving in the sleepy port of Muara Siberut at dawn following the overnight voyage from Sumatra, the students are warmly welcomed by their Mentawai guides and teachers. They set off after a hearty breakfast in outboard launches for the 4-5 hours it takes to navigate up the winding Siberut River and deep into the island's interior where Mentawai culture is most intact.

The students will spend the next 4-5 nights living with their Mentawai host families in traditional 'umas' – large, open air clan houses based on patrilineal descent. So as not to offend their hosts, proper protocol and Mentawai taboos are the first lessons to be learned. Men and women are assigned different sleeping areas of the 'uma' as sexual relations between them is taboo within the clan house. There are also gender-based taboos and privileges surrounding certain activities. Only men, for instance, weave the chicken baskets (roigets), make arrow poisons and take part in ritual hunts. Women hold the prerogatives of fishing in the rivers with dip nets, and tending the taro patches. It is taboo for a man to even set foot in a Mentawai woman's enclosed taro compound.

tree can feed a family of five for eight to nine months. The students try to imagine their own parents earning the income for eight to nine months of food from a single day's labor.

Sitting around oil lamps in the 'uma' at night, the Mentawai share their ancient legends with the students. They recount the story of the first earthquake, the cause of tsunamis, the first monkey, the origin of the sago tree, and many amusing tales of turtles, lizards, deer, monkeys and snails that like to play tricks on one another.

The students learn of the Mentawai's ancient spirituality – Jayarak – the sago palm as a 'tree of life'. They can see how the Sikeri, the shaman, over the course of their lives completely tattoo their bodies to resemble this sacred tree – their arms to resemble the fronds, their thighs to match the patterns on the sago tree trunk, and their chests and neck to symbolize the sago flower. Because sago trees grow from sucker shoots there is no need to plant or

Each day of the Mentawai study program brings new adventures and hands-on learning experiences. The girls might fashion their own skirts out of jungle leaves and follow the women down to the river to dig for clams with their toes, and turn over rocks in fast flowing creeks to catch crab, crayfish and eels in small dip nets. Meanwhile the boys join the men deep in the forest to gather secret ingredients for arrow poisons and to pound bark into tapa fabric to make their own loin cloths.

Everyone takes part in sago processing, though the men usually take on the heavier tasks like felling the sago palm, grating it to pulp, and stomping the fiber to release the starch. Women and girls help haul the baskets of raw pulp to the processing platform beside a water source. They also fashion the containers for the finished product from the blades of the very tree they have harvested. The genius of Mentawai technology shines through in making sago as every part of the tree is utilized in the process.

It only takes a day to process a sago tree and the starch it provides forms the main carbohydrate in the Mentawai's diet. A single

tend to them; when one is harvested another grows up in its place. It is truly a perpetual tree of life, a source of both physical and spiritual nourishment for these forest dwellers. Without sago palms, the students come to realize, the Mentawai could not maintain the population density or state of health they have so long enjoyed.

The Mentawai have advanced animal husbandry to a high art form. During their days living in the 'umas', with a menagerie of critters under the floorboards and roosting in the rafters, the students come to realize how much chickens and pigs are part of a Mentawai family. They also have opportunities to learn of the astonishing array of edible fruits and medicinal plants found in the Mentawai's forest gardens. If there's a budding ethno botanist among the students, this is virgin territory for study.

Watching the Mentawai Sikeri administer to the sick, the students have an opportunity to witness a people believed to have the highest ratio of doctors to patients of any society in the world. Indonesia has one medical doctor for every 6,786 people; the Mentawai have one traditional healer for every four people.

The Mentawai study program engages students as never before. Not only are the senses and brain bombarded with new experiences and impressions, but the students' bodies get a good work out too. Trekking through the rainforest in ankle-deep mud is tough at first for the prissy and privileged, but then there's the sudden reward of a paradise-like waterfall and a refreshing shower. It may be initially awkward to retreat to the jungle for toilet purposes, but the sweetest of flower perfumes fill the air with their fragrance to welcome you.

In addition to all the cultural lessons there's lots of time for play – frolicking in the mud with Mentawai children on the river bank, paddling dug-out canoes down the river, collecting exquisite sea shells along an unspoiled beach and snorkeling over coral reefs in crystalline waters. It's all Mentawai magic; there's no other educational experience quite like it.

gether the house frame, and the fan palms that need to be gathered from deep in the jungle to construct the roof and walls. Learning the ingenious method of securing palm blades between slats of split bamboo to form a waterproof roof, impresses everyone, but there are other lessons besides the techniques.

"Be certain all the palm blades are secured with their shiny side up," a Moken teacher tells the students through a translator, "otherwise lightening could strike this house."

The extent to which myth and magic permeates every aspect of Moken life becomes increasingly apparent to the students as they set out to harvest foods from the sea. "We do not need to see you today, shark," one of the Moken teachers intones before he plunges over the side of the boat to show the students how to gather clams, crab, and impale fish with a three-pronged spear along the reef shallows.

Moken Immersion

Students that take part in the Moken education program have equal opportunities for recreational adventures while delving deep into the traditional way of life of the celebrated 'Sea Gypsies'. The Moken are the indigenous peoples of the Mergui Archipelago in Myanmar and the offshore islands of Thailand's Andaman Coast. True seafarers, they lead a semi-nomadic lifestyle – living as nuclear family units aboard houseboats called 'kabangs' in the dry season (November-April) and settling in communal villages built along the beach during the stormy months (May-October).

Students that take part in the Moken Immersion study have opportunities to experience both styles of homes, and even help to construct a shelter of their own with just the materials Nature provides them. Wood for the elevated house pilings is cut from saplings or foraged from driftwood along the beach. The students are shown which liana vines can be pounded into rope to lash to-

The Moken are superb divers and can hold their breath underwater longer than almost any other people. Their knowledge of marine life easily surpasses that of the best marine biologists. When students leaf through a book illustrating more than 2,000 species of fish found in these waters, they are amazed to see that the Moken can name every one of them in their language, tell where to find them and what they taste like.

Moken legends, that have helped their people survive countless tsunamis, are shared with the students. They learn from one story why the Moken are shy to encounter a pig-tail macaque on the islands. These monkeys are said to have challenged and beaten the Moken in a swimming race in the early dawn of time, and the Moken take great pride in their swimming ability.

There are scores of lessons to learn on the Surin Islands where the students camp on a spectacular sandy beach and enjoy snorkeling over the largest expanse of hard corals in Thailand. Sometimes the Moken show the students which beach plants they can crush to make a poultice for an infected wound, or which saps they can extract to relieve the pain of a jellyfish sting. One night the students are taken out by boat to study the constellations and learn of the Moken's extraordinary ability to navigate by the stars. Recounting the ancient Moken stories associated with each cluster of stars holds the students spellbound.

The students are shown wooden totem poles representing Moken ancestors, and share the joy of dancing to drums at a Moken beach ceremony. They come to know a people living in harmony with their islands, and one another – a people that are still illiterate but who hold great lessons for us all.

PART III
STEWARDSHIP

"The illiterate of the 21st century will not be those
who cannot read and write, but those
who cannot learn, unlearn, and relearn"

Alvin Toffler

Global Initiatives in Earth Restoration

Some biologists have estimated that it will take 30 million years to restore planet Earth to the richness of biodiversity we knew as children. It's a sobering statistic. Still, life as we know it is phenomenally resilient and - given half a chance - Nature flourishes.

Humans too have proven to be surprisingly adaptable and resilient to change. But with the growing global population we now need to become acutely aware of our collective impact upon the Earth, unlearn some of our bad habits, and relearn new ways of living sustainably.

Earth stewardship is the ultimate goal of environmental education. It needs to come about not as a chore, but as a joyous endeavor. Once students have become aware of environmental problems, developed a deep sense of belonging to the Earth and are inspired into action to protect it, Earth restoration springs from the heart.

Whether it's reforesting a mangrove or hillside, stabilizing an eroding slope, removing toxic oil globs from a shoreline, or rehabilitating a degraded fish stream, there are many ways for people of all ages to get physically involved.

Science and modern technology also play important roles in Earth restoration. Monitoring the health of a creek through macroinvertebrate studies, developing useful products from industrial waste, discovering a new solution to water pollution, or a bio-safe insecticide are all ways in which young people are already proving themselves Earth stewards.

Stewardship activities do more than help us restore a healthy relationship with Nature, they help us restore relationships with one another. As we engage in cooperative rather than competitive exercises with a group of kindred spirits, the fulfillment experienced in conducting Earth stewardship projects expands exponentially.

This section of the book presents but a few of the many examples throughout the world where student/teacher initiatives are truly making a difference. Be inspired!

Beautifying a Bombay Byway (India)

Overcoming opposition and struggling through bureaucracy is all part of the challenge when a teacher steps out of the classroom with a daring plan to get students back in touch with Nature.

Like most class conscious societies, parents don't send their children to the most prestigious schools in Bombay because they want them to be getting dirt under their fingernails. The very thought of a child kneeling on the ground, pulling weeds, planting flowers and pruning trees is anathema to most financially privileged families. This is work for low-paid laborers and groundskeepers, not the nation's future business leaders, professors, scientists, doctors, lawyers and government officials.

So imagine the resistance when a teacher at an international school tries to initiate an environmental program that puts kids back in touch with themselves, each other and the natural world by creating a schoolyard park.

Jake Slodki, the science specialist at the American School of Bombay (ASB) in India, faced just such a social class dilemma, but overcame all opposition in a bold beautification program for his school. A long narrow and badly eroded hilltop that separates the properties of ASB and Ambani International School had caught Jake's attention as a possible location for an outdoor education program. Finding a patch of terra firma with green-up potential in an industrial city of 15 million is no simple task. The ridgeline was actually a boundary line separating two access byways to the neighboring schools, so it seemed unlikely real estate for any future expansion of either school's facilities.

Getting the students enthusiastic about the project and empowering them to play a lead role was only part of the challenge Jake faced. Staying focused and optimistic about the proposal, while wading through multiple levels of bureaucracy for final approval, was the more formidable task.

The students didn't just walk out of their classroom and start planting trees on Earth Day; there was a lot of preparatory work to be done first. Each student was required to

complete a Nature Journal survey of the area's flora and fauna using their five senses. "What am I seeing, hearing, touching, smelling, tasting?" Even that more elusive sixth sense was brought to play: "How do I feel being in this place?"

The students were next required to develop a food web for the local area determining, as best they could, what species of plants and animals were already present, how they interacted with one another, and how the students might be able to enhance this biodiversity through the re-introduction of species. Tree research was a crucial step in the process. The project wanted to plant native species, and so the students had to select those most suitable to the site. Drought resistance, sun and shade tolerance, benefits of a tree species to local birds and small mammals, and compatibility with other plants were all factors the students needed to take into consideration. From 52 possible trees first identified, the students narrowed their selection to 12 trees that met their rigid criteria for planting. A Microsoft Visio scale plan was then produced by the students for the type and location of each tree selected.

At last the students were ready to start beautifying their plot of land. To incorporate technology into the exercise, they were required to plot their planting points using two Global Positioning Systems to navigate the exact location for each plant. This activity offered a nice diversion for students that were more right-brained than green-thumbed.

Detailed procedures were followed of how to properly plant, water and care for each tree to ensure maximum survival rates.

The ASB Beautification Project is a long term rehabilitation project that will restore the entire hill over a period of time. By becoming stewards of their 'Peoples Park,' the students are not only creating a green space with aesthetic value for the whole community to enjoy, they are also transferring the values of stewardship to that community.

The educational benefits are multiple. The students are creating their own natural habitat to explore natural sciences and how humans interact with their environment. They are spending a healthy time outdoors where they can potentially engage multiple intelligences. They are learning about flora and fauna through locally knowledgeable people, and bridging the socio-economic chasm in Indian society between laborers and professionals. Most importantly, the students are experiencing a direct physical connection to the natural environment, developing a 'sense of place' and a spirit of stewardship in their school and surrounding community.

How many lesson plans achieve that?

A Bloomin' Good Idea
(Thailand)

Thai students transform marigold flowers into an environmentally-friendly, branded insecticide, and create their own future business along the way

It's not common for Asian educators to encourage their students to think "outside of the box". All too often rote memorization, unwavering discipline and religious adherence to rigid assignments characterize Thai education. But Mr. Amorpan Utsahagit, an economics teacher at Wittayakom School in Sukhothai, Thailand, has inspired twelve of his students to a level of achievement unprecedented in the Kingdom.

There is nothing about Wittayakom School that sets it apart from other Thai schools. It is large and overcrowded with an enrollment in excess of 3,000, and 50 students per class. It is also rural in nature, located in a farming district that grows rice, sugarcane, tobacco and marigolds. The school's location may be its only distinguishing feature. It is just down the road from the UNESCO World Heritage Site of ancient Sukhothai - the 700-year old center of the first Thai kingdom.

Mr. Amorpan Utasahagit is a teacher who embodies the best of his profession; he does not concede to mediocrity but encourages his students to excel in everything they do. When he challenged his economics class to develop a business plan that made a wiser use of locally available resources - turning something wasteful into something profitable - a team of twelve rose to the occasion.

It only took a few brainstorming sessions for the student team to turn their attention to marigolds – a flower grown commercially for use in floral arrangements, offerings at Buddhist shrines, and as garlands worn by Thai boxers before and after major bouts. The marigold is a short-lived plant that survives only a few days after flowering, and not all blooms are large and suitable for market. Recognizing the volume of waste in the industry, the students started to research the plant's properties.

For weeks they gathered to compare their research findings. Interviews with local farmers had yielded some valuable information. Marigolds emit a strong odor that repels insects; they have long been used as companionate plants to protect organic vegetable gardens.

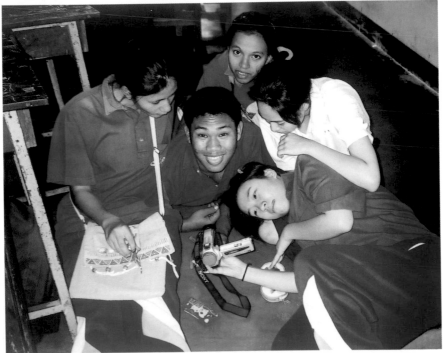

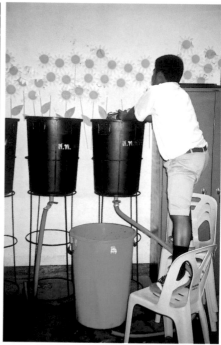

Research at the library was equally rewarding; marigolds possess a biochemical substance that kills certain insect pests. The students decided to try manufacturing their own eco-friendly insecticide.

As many of the team members were from local farming families they were not at all adverse to some heavy field work. Gathering up the marigold plants actually turned into a fun-filled class outing. Production involved the simplest of technologies. The plants were put through meat grinders to extract the liquid at a ratio of 80% flowers to 20% leaves and stems. Brown sugar, extracted from locally grown sugar palms, was added to the liquid to start a fermentation process. After 15 days of storage in plastic garbage bins the brew was ready to bottle. The students bottled their homemade insecticide in one liter plastic bottles and labeled it with their own brand name – 'Knockdown'.

Muay Thai (Thai boxing) is the revered national sport of Thailand and it is a time-honored tradition for champion boxers to enter and exit the ring wearing garlands of jasmine and marigold flowers. A knockdown in a Muay Thai bout is a huge crowd pleaser, and the students were hoping that their product would prove as popular with local tobacco farmers – all ardent boxing fans.

The marketing plan was simple at first. The students took their product home to their farmer parents and assumed that they would use it. They also employed a direct marketing strategy by discounting the product 20% to a salesperson for every 10 bottles sold. At the peak of the project, production capacity was an impressive 450 liters per day, but there were also set backs.

The students were dismayed to discover that because none of their potential customers had ever heard of Knockdown, they were reluctant to try it. The petrochemical industry, with its slick television advertising, had already cornered Thailand's insecticide market with expensive but environmentally destructive products that threatened farmers' health. Still, the students refused to concede defeat in their business plan. Taking a tip from the 'snake oil' vendors at local fairs, they came up with a witty marketing trick of

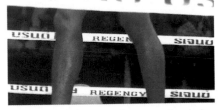

their own - giving away free samples during a road show through the countryside. It worked! More and more farmers started talking about Knockdown, expanding the market through word-of-mouth advertising.

Eventually 1,000 liters of Knockdown were sold at 100 baht (US$2.50) per bottle. Farmers found the product to be just as effective, and far more economical than multinational branded insecticides priced four to five times higher. Best of all Knockdown posed no health hazards to the farmers, nor did it leave toxic residues on the tobacco leaves or in the ground.

Panjapa Norathee (18), one of the students in charge of marketing and public relations, said the team members were taught to continually monitor the SWOT (strength, weakness, opportunity and threat) of their fledgling business, and thus devise ways to address weaknesses. Before determining the selling price, for instance, students had to calculate all their costs, most of which was incurred in production, packaging, transport and manpower. Still, the profit margin was a healthy 30%.

Since completion of the project, a number of companies have approached the team to commercially produce Knockdown. But the students' business savy has already extended well beyond their school project. They now have a patent pending on their product and have officially registered the brand name, intending to go into business together when they complete their formal schooling.

On July 24, 2003 the student team and their teacher were honored at a gala award ceremony in Bangkok presided over by Thailand's Minister of Finance. Their project titled: "Marigold - The Beauty that Can Boast its Useful Property" was chosen from 600 school projects as the best fresh idea in the Kingdom. A cash award of 400,000 baht (US$10,000) was given to their school as first prize in a national competition, and the students themselves shared the substantial profits from their venture.

A simple golden flower idea had become a gold mine for learning, financial return and future employment opportunity. More importantly, it has become a shining example of how young minds, with a little encouragement and guidance, can contribute to the future health of our planet.

The 'Breakfast Paper'
(Costa Rica)

The Age of Information is using more paper and consuming more trees than ever before, but a Costa Rican College, dedicated to Earth stewardship, has found a local solution in recycling the residue of local cash crops: banana, coffee and tobacco.

It sounds like a typical Costa Rican breakfast: the compulsory beans and rice, a thick, black (stand your hair straight up) coffee, a ripe banana and a good hand-rolled Honduran stogie to lull away the morning hours. But students at Earth University are now using most of the items to create their own brand name eco paper – proving in the end "you can have your breakfast and read it too."

Never short on new ideas or innovation, Costa Rica is one of the smallest countries on Earth, but it has carved out for itself a respected place in the world body of nations. Costa Rica's constitution, for instance, does not allow for the formation of an army; instead the country boasts the world's only University of Peace. The nation also protects its staggering biodiversity with a land allocation plan that does not allow a land owner to develop more than 20% of their property. Instead, the government offers considerable compensation to landowners that protect their land in a natural state. Thus, while most countries are steadily losing natural habitat for wildlife, Costa Rica is increasing theirs.

Putting environment at the forefront of national policy, Costa Rica created the world's first Earth University in 1990. EARTH was set up in the lush Atlantic lowlands several hours drive from the capitol of San Jose. It is a private, international, non-profit university offering education in agricultural sciences and natural resources with a goal of "contributing to sustainable development in humid tropics." Students come from all over, but tend to be from disadvantaged rural backgrounds in Latin America, Africa and Spanish-speaking Europe.

The research at EARTH seeks to "contribute to the development of sustainable systems focused on agricultural processes." So when students were presented with the challenge of making their own paper, they naturally turned to waste products from Central American cash crops.

Costa Rica is world famous for banana production, but stalk and leaf fiber from harvesting creates a 230,000 ton per year by-product that poses an ecological threat to the region. Adding banana fiber to post consumer paper seemed a good place to start in saving trees.

It was later discovered that for every one ton of cigar fiber used in paper production, 17 trees could be saved. The cigar fiber is processed in nearby Honduras and converted into paper by the school without the use of harmful chemicals.

Even coffee residue was converted to paper. Coffee paper is made by mixing recycled paper with actual brewed coffee and coffee skins, a left over by-product of the coffee plantations in El Salvador. Both agricultural by-products of the coffee plantations and the post consumer paper used in the mix create serious solid waste problems throughout Latin America.

Earth University produces a wide range of paper products that can be purchased via the Internet. These include: personal stationary, school supplies, office accessories, laser paper and envelopes. Better yet, a percentage of each sale goes towards a scholarship fund to support young leaders from Latin America that want to study sustainable development at EARTH.

Creative, sustainable paper production is just one of the spin-off benefits of the many research programs now underway at the university. Finding environmental solutions for today's problems, by tomorrow's leaders, is quintessential eco-education.

www.costaricanatural.com

 BANANA PAPER

 CIGAR PAPER

 COFFEE PAPER

Europe's Brave New Eco-Schools (Belgium)

Not content to merely recycle pop cans and paper, or plant a tree on Earth Day - the environmental rut many schools seem stuck in - some European schools are building a brave new world of eco-education right from the ground up.

"You are going to face a lot of opposition from teachers who don't want to change," cautions eco-school guru Sven Aerts, a self-proclaimed 'Engineer for the People.' Sven is a specialist in solar empowered systems, rainwater recuperation, and point-of-use water treatment and filtration. Based in Brussels, Belgium, near the European Commission and Parliament, Sven Aerts has been one of the creative people at the forefront of Europe's quiet eco-school revolution since its inception.

"It started slowly," says Sven, "when some students, parents, teachers and administrators left the traditional school system and started their own alternative eco-school. They received a lot of criticism at first, but eventually their persistence and success opened the minds of others. The big break came when some rich private schools converted and that in turn inspired the European Commission to further propagate the concept."

Today, good examples of eco-schools can be found in Austria, Belgium and the Netherlands. They are sometimes newly built schools, but more often tend to be renovated or reconverted ones. The goal is not only to conserve energy and natural resources but to have the school building and grounds actually become a didactic place for teachers and students to better understand their place in the nature of things.

On the roof of buildings, solar collectors are installed that heat or cool the school walls and floor, depending upon the need. In temperate latitudes, for instance, copper tubing can be placed in the floor and walls. This radically reduces heating costs. Better yet, the students have no need to enter the building with shoes anymore. Like the custom of leaving ones shoes at the doorstep of an Asian home, the relaxed, homey feeling of stockinged feet has been found to be more conducive to learning.

Most opposition to employing solar collectors stems from the costs involved, but Europe's eco-schools have found a clever way to get a 100% return on their investment within six years and start turning a profit thereafter. In the summer months when school is not in session, photovoltaic cells are used to harness the intense energy of the summer sun. The school sells this unneeded electricity back to the grid of the local electrical company. Because the school only sells at peak hours, when demand is the highest, they get the best possible price for their energy.

Engineers help the teachers with technical knowledge until they can take up the subject in their curricula. As Sven says, "For most teachers, it has been 10 or 15 years since they left university; they are good in peda-

gogy but need some bridging between their disciplines and the engineering part of the school."

Thermometers in solar collectors, or the photovoltaic system, read out amperage per hour to a computer. Engineers instruct teachers how to set up the output of the measuring instruments on a computer that can show electricity production on-line through the school's website. It is common for teachers, students and even headmasters to periodically check the website during summer holidays to see how much money they have made on any given day selling electricity.

Water conservation through recycling is another major discipline at eco-schools. Rainwater is harvested via the roofs of buildings and surfaced grounds. The roof water is collected in large transparent buffer bins that hang in the school lavatories. In this way children can see that when it is raining the level goes up, but when they flush a toilet it goes noticeably down. They are thus educated in the basics of water conservation: to close taps while lathering hands with soap, to close taps completely after washing, and to care about leaky faucets. Gold fish, or other hardy species, are often housed in these water storage bins to further drive home the lesson of water conservation. Unnecessary toilet flushing or wastefully running of taps is unlikely to occur if the school's pet fish are getting low on water.

Underground storage units are used to collect rain runoff from sidewalks, roadways, parking areas and paved playgrounds. These reservoirs are then used for watering an eco-school's garden. Herbs, vegetables, medicinal plants and endangered native species are all propagated here. Fruiting trees that attract a host of pollinators and provide food for birds, small mammals and humans are used in place of purely ornamental species. Water reclamation from school bio-sewage treatment also takes place at advanced stages of an eco-school's evolution.

An eco-school never rests on its laurels but constantly strives to grow "greener" every year. School clubs compete with teachers and one another to constantly evaluate the effectiveness of projects and initiate new ones; it is a never-ending dance of disciplines. A biology teacher, for instance, might start using the school's composting system, built by a school club, to offer class lessons in decomposition and the myriad species that are decomposers. An eco-club might use the compost to grow organic bio-food in the school garden that is sold at a premium in the school cafeteria to support other eco projects. A lot of the little pieces of the puzzle start to fall into place in students' minds; they become a lot less divorced from the cycles of Nature and come to share an intimate sense of being connected to other living things.

Currently, the European Commission is supporting four eco-school initiatives - two in Europe and two worldwide. There is also a national network deployed for eco-schools in many European countries. It is up to the schools and students to decide if they want to participate.

Taking bold steps can initially seem risky in any venture. An eco-school initiative certainly moves a school body out of the over-consumer comfort zone the developed world has become all too comfortable with. But if education is really to be the vanguard of change it purports to be, there is no better place for a teacher, student or administrator than at that leading edge.

Jakarta International School (left) puts students in touch with Nature with every change of class. Covered outdoor walkways, that shed frequent tropical downpours, are used to connect classroom modules. Drinking water coolers are conveniently stationed along the way for students to refill their own water bottles. Ponds, full of aquatic life, invite students to explore Nature on their own during free time.

Eco-schools needn't be high tech. A hill tribe school in Northern Thailand (above) gives a whole new meaning to the term 'eco-school'. Built with locally available and biodegradable materials, and naturally air conditioned by hilltop breezes, this classroom puts students in touch with Nature in ways a high-tech 'eco-school' could never dream of.

Sea Shell Solutions
(Canada)

Three high school students in Halifax, Nova Scotia find an alternative method to improve water quality using the simplest biotechnology possible - scallop shells.

It is often said that the simplest solutions are the best, but who would ever have thought that three high school students would stand sewage treatment technology on its head with a single class experiment?

J.L. Ilsley High School in Halifax, Nova Scotia, is not exactly noted for academic excellence in innovative solutions, nor is it much of a "green" school. Not far from its hallowed halls, the City of Halifax dumps 180 million liters of sewage each day into Halifax Harbor, a legacy of abuse that dates back 250 years to the time the first immigrants arrived here from Europe. The city is not necessarily proud of this tradition and it has been

looking at ways to clean up its act, but how? Technologies exist to get the job done, but the estimated cost of $300 million dollars is enough to scare any taxpayer right out of town, or force them to overthrow their elected government, and no one on City Council wants to see that. Enter Amy Trottier, Elias Fares and James Beaton-Johnson, three grade 11 students from Ilsley H.S. with a seemingly all too simplistic solution. Why not use refuse from Nova Scotia's bivalve fishery to filter toxins from water through microscopic spaces in shells?

A pig farmer living along the coast of Japan discovered the possible application of shells in water treatment by happy accident. When he started discarding oyster shells in a pond repeatedly soiled by his pigs he was utterly amazed to see the water become visibly cleaner within days. The three Nova Scotia students decided to expand on this concept using in vitro and in vivo experiments. They selected two polluted sites for their study,

Halifax Harbor and the main river running through town - the McIntosh Runs.

There had been many school clean-up attempts of McIntosh Runs as part of Earth Day activities over the years, but these simply consisted of the removal of rubber tires, shopping carts and other eyesores. They did nothing to improve water quality, to reduce dissolved particles, dissolved cations from metals and other contaminants: road salt, acid rain, car wash fluids, sewage, as well as commercial and industrial waste products. The three students were hopeful that their experiments might address this greater issue.

Before starting their experiment the three students tested both harbor and river water samples for turbidity, acidity, conductivity and temperature, and they repeated the same battery of tests at 24-hour intervals once the scallop shells were added. All numbers improved dramatically. Within one day, fecal coliform counts in harbor water samples fell from 50,000 parts per liter to just 1,300 parts - safe enough for swimming.

"We didn't think the shells would work when we first started," said James Beaton-Johnson. "Now we don't know what the limits are." The students believe that not only does the calcium carbonate in the shells chemical structure help to neutralize acidic waters, but microscopic spores in the shell surface also act as filters to absorb harmful bacteria and dissolved toxins. It wasn't until they persuaded a local university to have a look at the surface of scallop shells through an electron force microscope that it became clearly evident that they could function as a filter.

The Mayor of Halifax was so impressed with the research that he offered the three budding scientists positions on the Halifax Harbor Clean Up Project. They also received the first-ever Institute for Marine Biosciences Youth Fellowship Award and placed second at the 2002 Aventis Biotech Challenge. When word got back to Japan that these students had seized on an idea from a mere Japanese news report, they were invited as honorary guests to attend the World Water Forum in Kyoto.

The three clever students are looking into patenting the process they developed and may well have created new careers for themselves. By thinking well outside the box, they have inadvertently stumbled upon a possible age-old but lost secret, for they now speculate that anthropologists have completely misinterpreted aboriginal shell middens found along the coast. What academics assure us are prehistoric refuse dumps, the students believe were pits used to purify water for aboriginal drinking purposes.

The truth of this hypothesis may never be fully known, but these three school kids have already left the world a lasting legacy. From a local river that needs cleaning, to a third world country with inadequate drinking water, the safe, inexpensive, environmentally friendly procedure they developed could benefit plants, animals and human beings for many years to come.

Sumatran Seed Bank
(Indonesia)

Fifty students at an oil company school in Indonesia took on an environmental stewardship project that even the world's largest conservation group couldn't handle. Inspired by a passionate teacher, they set out to save the genetic diversity of the richest rainforest on Earth.

Cal Tex American School near Pekanbaru, Sumatra, is not the place an environmental advocacy group would expect to find a green project of global significance. Aren't oil companies, after all, the enemy - responsible for some of the worst ecological disasters of our time? And how could a school of only fifty elementary and middle school students, and a single high school student, achieve anything of real significance anyway? The answer lies in the devotion of a single teacher, Terry Donohue, his committed students, and the team of professional support he built around a bold school initiative.

Cal Tex American School has been educating the sons and daughters of oil company employees since WWI when the American giant drilled its first wells in oil-rich Sumatra. Back then this sixth largest island in the world was covered in an unbroken expanse of tropical rainforest, part of the oldest and richest terrestrial ecosystem on our planet. Over the past few decades, that great green mantle and the myriad species that depend upon it have been reduced to mere fragments through logging and uncontrolled land clearing by burning.

In 1998 the World Wide Fund for Nature identified a remnant patch of forest, not far from the Cal Tex complex, as having the greatest botanical diversity on Earth. A staggering 200 species of vascular plants could be found in a single square meter of this forest; it was many times richer in species than the most diverse areas of the Amazon.

Tragically, illegal logging operations were steadily eating away at this preserve and it seemed just a matter of time before it would be completely lost. The Government of Indo-

224

still healthy stands of primary forest supporting complex communities of animals: hornbills, monkeys, gibbons, wild pig, deer and even tapir. The plan was to use these natural gene bank reserves, and others in central Sumatra, to expand the forest base throughout the Cal Tex site.

It took many months to build and stock the great green house that the students came to know as "The Tree House." Annually growing more than 2,000 trees from 50 different species, this facility might well have been called "The First Gene Bank of Sumatra."

When the trees grew large enough to transplant, the school secured permission from the Cal Tex executive to plant them along the cleared right-of-ways throughout the extensive road network of the company complex. From 1999

nesia and the most powerful conservation groups in the world seemed helpless in trying to save it. The students of Cal Tex American School took on the challenge. They decided in 1999 to convert a substantial area of their schoolyard into a massive greenhouse complex in order to propagate as many species of trees as they could find in the native forest. They used both class time and after school hours for forays into the forest where they learned to gather, identify and ultimately propagate more than fifty tree species.

In addition to the housing complexes, recreation center and golf course that make up the private land holdings of Cal Tex in Sumatra, there are

to 2002, the students planted a staggering 6,000 trees on the site. They deliberately left sufficient space between their plantings to allow for other wind-borne species and seeds carried by birds, bats and monkeys to colonize areas on their own. This strat-

egy would result in a more natural mix of trees than human effort alone could produce.

As the project gained more and more momentum there was talk of reforesting the golf course with native species and requesting Cal Tex to turn the entire complex into an international botanical research center when the oil runs out in the not too distant future.

Not content with merely picking up litter and recycling paper and pop cans, as do most schools, this little-school-that-could wanted to make a bigger difference in the world, and they did. Their "Tree House" project is more than green; it is globally significant.

Few teachers seem willing to break out of their comfort zones in taking on a project of this magnitude, vision and scope. But the rewards are immeasurable for the students, the prospects for humanity's future more hopeful, and it is to the everlasting credit of those daring teachers that do.

There's My Salmon!
(USA)

Washington State elementary school students transform a dead waterway near their school into a healthy creek for salmon reproduction; they enroll their parents, neighbors and City Council in the process.

The year is 1987 and Tom Murdoch, Executive Director of the Adopt-A-Stream Foundation near Everest, Washington, is showing off recently rehabilitated Pigeon Creek to ABC's Home Show television crew. A group of fifth grade students are also at the creek side to add cute human interest to the story. Four years earlier these same students had nurtured juvenile salmon from eggs in an aquarium in their first grade classroom and released them in the creek. There had been no salmon run in Pigeon Creek for 28 years and the likelihood of these few fish surviving the four thousand in one odds to make their way to sea and back was virtually nil.

As the TV cameras were rolling and Tom Murdoch was waxing eloquently about the need to protect salmon habitat, he suddenly

was interrupted by a fifth grade boy shouting, "There's my salmon! There's my salmon!!" Suddenly all the kids started shouting, "Wow, look at that fish, that's our fish!" Somehow, against all odds, the grade one student project had proven a total success. The first salmon were returning to Pigeon Creek in nearly three decades and the historic moment was being recorded on camera for all America to see.

How did these kids do it? With a lot of commitment, hard work and the support of an entire community they inspired to help them.

Brandon King, the fifth grade teacher at Jackson Elementary School recalled from his youth how the salmon used to be so thick in Pigeon Creek, "You could walk across on their backs." But a shopping center development in the headwaters of the creek in 1958 put an end to that. Forests and wetlands were lost under new rooftops, parking lots and roads. That resulted in increased volume and flow of water during the rainy season that eroded stream banks. Sediment from the eroded stream banks, washed downstream, smothering spawning gravels and wiping out the salmon.

The salmon run had disappeared for so long that few believed the creek could be rehabilitated. Inspired by the work of the Adopt-A Stream Foundation, Jackson Elementary School established a long-term goal to restore the salmon run to Pigeon Creek. It would not be a straight forward task. They had to design a 20-year action plan that started with a watershed inventory and monitoring the health of the stream. Macro invertebrate (underwater insects) and water quality studies were conducted as part of class sessions to determine the relative health of the watershed for fish growth and reproduction.

In addition to the scientific analysis, the students also played an important advocacy role. They produced their own map showing their creek, its surrounding watershed, and several land use features. Students also reprinted flyers produced jointly by the Adopt-A-Stream Foundation and the Washington State Department of Ecology entitled: "Streams: Guidelines for Survival". The students then set out to distribute their map and flyer reprint to every household and business in the watershed with a plea to read the information and to play an active role in

the community effort to restore Pigeon Creek's salmon run.

The students were getting more and more charged up about their mission. They conducted community stream clean-ups. They spray painted stencils in front of storm drains that flow into Pigeon Creek with the message: "Dump No Waste, Drains to Stream." And as a symbolic gesture, in 1983, they released the few hundred salmon fry they had raised in their classroom aquariums into the creek.

But there was really much more to be done. Pigeon Creek was still a long way from being a healthy fish habitat, and the Jackson School students knew they would have to influence change at higher levels. They prepared a slide show of their activities that they presented to the Everett City Council, and asked the city to address the storm water runoff problem that had led to the demise of the salmon in the first place.

Following the high profile meeting, a group of teachers, parents and concerned citizens formed the Everett Streamkeepers that began to monitor all land use proposals in the

After the national media coverage surrounding the successful return of the first salmon in 1987, the city made good on its promise to the students. It designed and constructed a storm water control pond in the Pigeon Creek headwaters near the shopping Center. As a result of the student lobbying effort, the City of Everett spent half a million dollars on a project to improve Pigeon Creek's salmon-spawning habitat. Kids made it happen!

Almost everyone has an environmental horror story to tell, but Jackson Elementary students were determined to put a fairy tale happy ending on theirs.

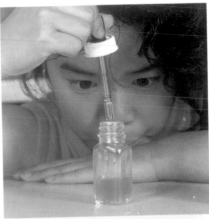

watershed. Through their diligence, a major subdivision proposal that would have impacted Pigeon Creek was significantly altered. The revised plan featured vegetation buffers and storm-water bio-filtration strategies. The new environmentally conscious design proved very profitable for the developer who named the new subdivision "The Preserve" and won the Governors "Environmental Excellence Award."

Earth Ceremonies

For most of human existence our ancestors worshipped, or at least recognized an essential relationship with, the elements of earth, air, fire and water. Indigenous peoples, with strong animistic traditions, still pay homage to these elements through rituals and ceremonies that serve to unite members of a tribe in common purpose.

Perhaps humanity at large needs a more cohesive sense of identity where we see ourselves less as members of nations, religions, political parties, race or ethnicity, and more in terms of a planetary community. Given our sheer numbers, such a shared identity might ultimately prove necessary to our survival.

What are the things we have in common that should serve to unite us? Well, we all breathe the same air and secure our food nourished by the same earth. Water makes up the vast majority of our bodies and covers two thirds of our planet. Humans and life in general certainly could not survive without it. And then there is the most basic element of all - fire.

From the "Big Bang" that scientists believe created the universe, to the countless stars that stud the night sky, fire is the most primal element of all. There could be no life on Earth without the fire that burns in our sun, providing the energy for photosynthesis, and humans might still be little different from other primates had we not developed an ability to create and control fire.

At the turn of the millennium there was a media generated moment that profoundly affected most of the world's population. As global news networks recorded millennium celebrations around the world, moving their coverage from one time zone to the next as the clock struck midnight, there was a powerful sense that we were all connected. What if we could achieve that same sense of unity by honoring and celebrating something far more tangible and important to our survival than the Western calendar?

Full moons are times in the monthly calendar that affects us all, even when we're not always willing to admit it. Summer and winter solstices, as well as autumn and spring equinoxes, are other significant calendar events because they mark our planetary position in its elliptical orbit around the sun. What if events like this could be used quarterly for globally recognized ceremonies that honor the elements without offending any religious, cultural or national sensibilities? We already have an internationally recognized Earth Day; why not also have an Air Day, a Fire Day, and a day to recognize the supreme importance of water?

Interestingly enough, there are already a number of cultural events that could serve as models for what these celebrations might look like. Take water, for example. It would be hard to find a more beautiful ceremony to show respect to water than Thailand's time-honored tradition of Loy Krathong. Seven hundred years ago, in the first Thai Kingdom of Sukhothai, a woman in the royal court is said to have created a beautiful 'krathong' - a float made from the cross section of a banana stalk. She decorated this circular, chambered float with elaborately folded banana leaves, flowers, joss sticks and candles, then knelt down beside the waters of a temple pond to float it. Giving thanks for a year of ample rainfall, bountiful rice crops and an abundance of fish, and asking forgiveness for all the bad people do to water throughout the year, the woman released her 'krathong' upon the water. The little ceremony so charmed King Ramkhamhaeng that he instructed all of his subjects to revere water in the same way on the full moon of the 10th lunar month.

Seven centuries later, Loy Krathong is still religiously celebrated throughout Thailand on the full moon in November when water levels are at their highest with the close of the rainy season. Before releasing a 'krathong', the Thai people place fingernail and hair clippings amidst the flowers as a way of releasing bad energy, but also in recognition of the fact that water comprises over 70% of our bodies. A bit of raw rice and a pinch of salt are added, because without water we could neither grow nor cook our food. Finally, a few Thai baht coins are placed among the flowers to symbolize the fact that water is more precious than all the money in the world.

To see 70 million Thais transcend their political, ethnic and religious differences through honoring the spirit of water, on the magical full moon night of Loy Krathong, is to see the powerful potential for Earth ceremonies to unite humanity in common purpose. For many years now, the *Reefs to Rainforests* program in Thailand has been doing 'krathong' ceremonies with international school students as part of the closing ceremony. It is not only a cultural immersion experience for these students, but a transformational one; for the first time in most of their lives these students are approaching water with reverence.

Earth, air and fire ceremonies are also practiced by many cultures throughout the world. Our ancestors have performed planting and harvest ceremonies since the advent of agriculture. These activities continue to this day in some societies. Consider the Royal Plouging Ceremony in Thailand, the Hopi Corn Ceremonies in New Mexico, harvest festivals held throughout Europe, or the North American Thanksgiving Day. One of the most common ways in which students worldwide mark Earth Day is by planting a fruit tree – a good choice for honoring our dependence on the soil and the bounty of foods the earth provides for us.

An "Air Day" celebration would not be that difficult to imagine. Kites immediately spring to mind. With the exception of certain fundamentalist regimes in the world, determined to remove the last ounce of joy from life, kite flying is an activity enjoyed by most societies. Kites for an "Air Day" ceremony could be designed in the shapes of all the creatures of the air: from birds to bats, butterflies to dragonflies. Others could be painted with messages for clean air, depict various types of cloud formations, lightning bolts, tor-

nadoes, hurricanes, or even portray images of the ancient gods of thunder, wind and storms.

An alternative to kite flying for an "Air Day" ceremony might be the release of hot air balloons made of biodegradable materials. In Chiang Mai, Thailand, thousands of these balloons are set aloft during the annual Yi Ping festival. They are constructed of lightweight rice paper wrapped around a cylindrical frame made of thin strips of bamboo. A small fire, lit from candle wax or cotton soaked in kerosene, is wired to the bottom of the balloon for propulsion. These glowing lantern-balloons are most beautiful when released at night. As the hot air builds up within the balloons, they gently rise higher and higher into the cool night sky, creating a dazzling spectacle. Upper air currents, undetectable at ground level, become readily apparent as the lantern-balloons drift in that direction.

This type of ceremony could easily cross over to being an activity to mark "Fire Day", but there is no shortage of cultural models to draw inspiration from when it comes to fire. Fire festivals have ancient origins and fall throughout the year. Even Christmas, that marks the birth of Jesus, was shifted two months later to coincide with (and replace) the pagan solstice celebrations that marked the return of the sun.

Bonfires are used worldwide to highlight certain occasions. Norsemen still welcome the return of the sun god with Yule in December/January – a 24-day period of feasting, storytelling, and bonfires that culminate in the burning of a model Viking boat. In February bonfires are used to invoke returning power of the sun in Luxembourg. In March, fire walking is held in conjunction with Vernal Equinox observances in China, India, Sri Lanka and other parts of Southeast Asia. Summer Solstice (Midsummer's Eve) celebrations are held throughout Europe with bonfires and torch processions. Summer Solstice in the Northern Hemisphere is, of course, Winter Solstice in southern latitudes. In Peru and Bolivia, the Incas commemorated the same day by kindling a new fire with a concave mirror at the Golden Temple of the Sun to mark the occurrence of the sun's southernmost migration.

In China, the birth of the Fire God is celebrated on July 17. In Japan, August 16-17 marks Daimonji when bonfires are set ablaze on mountaintops; November 8 marks the Shinto Feast of bellows that honors the goddess of the hearth fire. Ethiopia has a lively torch parade and all-night bonfires on September 27 for their Maskal Festival and both the Hopi and Zuni tribes of North America hold New Fire Ceremonies in December.

Two of the greatest challenges in encouraging all humanity to come together in honoring the elements of earth, air, fire and water are to agree upon dates for each observance, and to ensure that the form the ceremonies take are respectful of cultural traditions and the environment. Bonfires, for instance, would not be appropriate in areas with fuel wood shortages. In Nepal, where wood cannot be so lavishly squandered, the Newari celebrate their Festival of Lights by placing tiny terra cotta oil lamps on every window sill of every house and temple. The effect is spectacular - a fairyland of lights. Candle lit processions are another way of creating fire magic without the large use of fire. Finding the most environmentally friendly way to celebrate an Earth, Air, Fire, and Water Day will become part of the educational challenge of each event.

If school groups started practicing these events it wouldn't take more than a generation or two for them to become institutionalized in societies at large. Global media could greatly influence these ceremonies, and the speed with which they catch on, by covering them as lead stories the four times each year they occur. These quarterly events are not meant to replace or impinge upon existing cultural expressions, but to add to the repertoire. Youth that have taken part in the *Rediscovery* program (pgs.178-187) over the past three decades, when asked what could be done to make the experience even more powerful for them, most commonly reply, "Have more ceremonies."

Ceremony is one of the things that most distinguish us as a species, not just the courtship rituals and group bonding exercises common to social animals, but large groups of people coming together to celebrate cyclical and conceptual cultural events. Rather than confuse the issue by coinciding Earth, Air, Fire and Water celebrations with solstice and equinox celebrations, which differ with the two hemispheres, it might be best to adhere to a lunar calendar because full moons occur on the same night throughout the world. The full moon in March could mark "Air Day", in June "Earth Day", in September "Water Day', and in December "Fire Day".

Celebrating our humanity through recognition of the elements that affect every one of us in our daily lives, and annually re-dedicating ourselves to respecting these elements, could do all of us a world of good.

235

"Those who dare to teach
should never cease to learn"
Pablo Freire
Brazilian educator

Teachers Tool Kit

Let's Go!

Now that you have made a personal commitment to teaching yourself and others as much as you can about Nature, you might need a few tools.

As a teacher at an institution - whether private, public, formal or informal - jumping through all the bureaucratic hoops to get something done can sometimes be disheartening. It might even stifle your creativity and kill your spirit. We hope that won't happen!

In this section we are providing a few examples of things to think about when you are implementing your new environmental education program.

These ideas are fluid and may or may not work at your school. Only you can be the judge of that. But they are tried and true and have worked for many.

This section of the book is designed to streamline the process for you. Don't recreate the wheel if you don't have to - use and adapt these ideas!

Writing a proposal for an outdoor classroom

If you want to implement an outdoor classroom at your school, there are a few essential steps that must be undertaken to achieve your goal.

You must at the very least:

1) propose the idea to administration
2) 'sell' the idea to colleagues
3) build and maintain the trails
4) train staff in methods of outdoor education (while this book doesn't cover that aspect, attending one of our week long courses will help you learn those skills!)
5) and most importantly, use those skills! Get your students outdoors and encourage other teachers to join you!

The Proposal:

If you're like many teachers, you don't necessarily like the bureaucracy and red tape that goes along with accomplishing something in your school. At times, even the simplest tasks can require endless paperwork and possibly presentations to administration, colleagues and students. It may be discouraging. You may even find yourself saying, "Why all the fuss? I just want to do something fun and good for the kids."

Try not to get frustrated to the point of giving up. Hopefully the following pointers will help. Also remind yourself that administrators are not your nemesis; they have important roles to play in the process to ensure student safety, security, allotting funds and other considerations that will be important in helping you realize your goal.

The proposal should:

• be short and to the point (2 pages max)
• be concise
• justify your idea and produce the following:
  1. a rationale (stating the overall reason you want to undertake this project)
  2. how the students will benefit
  3. how the teachers will benefit
  4. how the school will benefit
  5. how the environment will benefit

Proposal for implementing an outdoor classroom at (school name)
(date)
(proposed by)

> The rationale is a very important part of the proposal. It serves to inform administration that there is a need for the outdoor classroom.

Rationale:

Land adjacent to (school name) is available for use as an outdoor classroom. Several teachers have expressed interest in utilizing this space to enhance their lessons and allow them opportunities not afforded in a traditional educational setting. If implemented, the effects of an outdoor classroom and the lessons learned from the natural setting will prove to be an invaluable asset to the students, the school, the teachers and the community of (school name).

> CRUCIAL! Should be one of the main selling points to admin. and teachers. After all, we ALL want what is best for the kids!

Benefits for students:

> Notice how it ties into educational theory. Very important selling point on why this is something the school NEEDS to do.

- By being outdoors students can potentially engage multiple intelligence's (Gardner, 1983)
  - Bodily-Kinesthetic intelligence ("body smart")
  - Intrapersonal intelligence ("self smart")
  - Naturalist intelligence ("nature smart")
- Opportunities to learn local flora and fauna

> It seems that kids nowadays know more corporate logos than living organisms!

- Allow students to develop a 'sense of place' connected to their school and nearby Nature
- Learn from local experts
- Experience a direct physical connection to the natural environment (you simply cannot do this in a classroom!)

Benefits for the school: ← If it seems the school cannot function without doing this then **you're in!**

- Allow (school name) to fulfill their commitment to environmental awareness through teaching and learning
- Professional development opportunities for faculty and staff in methods of outdoor education
- Potential partnerships with local organizations
- (School name) can assume a leadership role in providing environmental education to the community
- Provide an opportunity to build a common thread throughout the K-12 curriculum

Benefits for the teacher:
- Opportunities to get outdoors into the 'natural laboratory' provided by nearby environs
- Provide a potential for different mediums and modes of instruction
- Professional development opportunities through workshops
- Teach to a wider array of the 8 different intelligences that are not easily addressed in the classroom (refers back to the educational theory mentioned earlier)
- Build relationships with local experts and organizations (some thing all schools, especially International Schools, should strive to do)

Benefits for the community:
- Students can become stewards for their environment and transfer these values to other community members
- Indirect benefits from green space and esthetic value of having undisturbed, regenerating forest nearby

Benefits for the Environment:
- An outdoor classroom will allow native plants and animals to re-establish themselves in and near campus. Since much of the land near campus is developed, this is crucial to allow them a 'safe haven' to live in a natural setting

Potential partnerships:
- List any organizations or individuals that might make a good partner

Tips for Working with Kids Outdoors

Determine the needs of your group
- Age, health conditions, physical and mental capabilities must be taken into consideration when formulating a good plan for the group.

Develop a plan
- Plan your lesson by using the outdoor setting to engage all the senses.

- Create an ebb and flow in your activities by using 'energy burners' to get rid of pent-up energy before beginning a more focused or reflective activity. Once the kids have relaxed they can focus better.

Find a safe location
- When using an outdoor location be aware of possible hazards (i.e. overhanging dead limbs, poisonous plants or venomous animals, rising tides, or flood prone rivers).

- It's always a good idea to visit your location ahead of time to make sure you can find it quickly with students, and that it's suitable for your activity (i.e. choosing an open, clear space or forest depends on what you plan to do).

Create a safe atmosphere
- Enter into the spirit of play (your enthusiasm becomes thiers), but never lose your self in the fun. Remember, as the leader you must constantly monitor the comfort level and personal safety of each participant.

243

- Be aware of sexual energies and signs of discomfort in mixed-gender activities, especially those involving touch or innuendo.

Come fully prepared

- Make a list of all the materials you'll need and make sure they are packed ahead of time.

- Keep it simple: blindfolds, species cards, string, index cards, a stick and pen and paper are all you'll need for most activities!

State the rules clearly

- It's always easier to be more firm at first and then ease up than vice versa.

- Keep rules simple, usually 3-5 in number; kids can be encouraged to come up with their own.

- Decide how you feel about live animals (i.e. some instructors allow students to catch live animals in order for them to interact with them directly while other instructors feel it causes unnecessary stress to the animal).

Be flexible and fair

- When using outdoor activities always have an alternative plan should there be a sudden change in weather or a condition beyond your control.

- Use your planned activities but recognize the need to change gears and do some thing completely different if the group's energy or interest changes.

- Have a few "canned" lessons for spontaneity on hand in case you see an unexpected animal or something interesting presents itself (i.e. If your activity is supposed to be about botany but a deer, turtle or snake appears, then by all means change your lesson to support what you see!)

- Kids have a profound sense of injustice; give every participant an opportunity to play, and be fair when subjective judgement is called for in choosing a 'winner!'.

- Welcome CHAOS and be ready to switch gears if a lesson takes a new direction or does not follow your plan.

- Try not to let one kid dominate by being aware of shy students and students in the back trying to see or hear.

Don't feed negativity

- Try to absorb, rather than combat, negative attitudes (i.e. Student: "This game is stupid! I'm not gonna play it!" Teacher: "That's fine, can you please help me lead the activity for the others to enjoy?").

Don't over do it

- Never force play or carry it beyond the group's physical or emotional levels of enjoyment. If there is a problem affecting the entire group, such as a strong accusation of unfair play, then a "cool down" period may be required (*Talking Feather* works well here – see pgs.144-145).

Don't lecture

- Introduce more formal information as introductions or closures to activities.

- Allow the kids to discover Nature and not be told about it directly from the instructor.

- Latin names are usually unnecessary since kids won't remember them.
- Go for an experience and not a 'lesson'.
- Stop and explore, use "teachable moments" when something presents itself.
- Add an element of suspense to your hike by beginning with a mystery or clue to what you might see, hear, touch or feel outside.
- Don't be afraid to say "I don't know".

Re-bond when closing

- Never end a session abruptly like a school bell recess time's up! Rather plan your closing to bring the group back together in a spirit of oneness. This provides an opportunity for group feedback, especially if the instructor has been doing all the talking!
- Be a good listener and listen to all their stories about how their "Dad one time caught a fish" even though your lesson is about plants.

Safety

Safety should always be a primary concern of an instructor whether indoors, in a laboratory or out on the trail. However, safety becomes of utmost concern when on the trail due to the unpredictable nature of conducting lessons outdoors. Every instructor should at least be certified in first aid and CPR and 'life guarding' if activities take place near water.

Lessons on the trail rarely lead to serious injury if the instructor is focused and safety conscious. In fact, most injuries are very minor and fall into the category of scrapes, bruises and stings. The old adage an ounce of prevention is worth a pound of cure

generally holds true for outdoor education. A perceptive instructor can sense when it is time to slow down and let participants cool down, which, in many cases prevents injuries.

Since environmental education is often associated with adventure, a wise instructor knows how to read a group and determine their capabilities and comfort levels in regard to performing tasks such as kayaking, canoeing, hiking, climbing and biking.

Before you go outside:

Make sure you check the following:
- Notify administrators, colleagues or friends of your whereabouts during the lesson (especially if you leave campus, visit a trail or go to a remote location).
- Equipment for lesson (clip boards, pencils, magnifying glass, string, species cards etc.)
- Drinking Water
- Mosquito repellent
- Snack
- Hat and sunscreen
- Binoculars
- Field guides (birds, plants, insects, etc.)
- Day pack for equipment
- First aid kit

Fun Facts and Mnemonic Devices

The following are interesting ways to help students remember information about Nature. The challenge is to devise your own or ask the students to invent a new way to remember fun facts! Give it a try!

What organisms live symbiotically to form a lichen:

"Freddy Fungus took a likin' (lichen) to Alice Algae. They decided to get married and now live happily ever after!"

The classification scheme for living things:

"Kind Pigs Come Over For Good Slop"
   Kingdom
   Phylum
   Class
   Order
   Family
   Genus
   Species

How to tell a grass from a reed and a sedge:

"Sedges have edges, reeds are round and grasses are segmented all the way to the ground."

In North America, to tell a venomous snake from a non-venomous snake remember the poem:

"Red next to yellow could kill a fellow; red next to black is a friend of Jack."

(In other words if you come across a snake that has red stripes next to yellow stripes it is venomous while a snake with red stripes next to black stripes is non-venomous).

Always keep in mind though, it's best to leave ALL snakes alone in the wild and not harass, disturb, pick up, or annoy them in any manner!

To never forget the order of the planets in our solar system from the sun just remember:

My Very Eager Mother Just Sent Us Nine Pizzas.

   Mercury
   Venus
   Earth
   Mars
   Jupiter
   Saturn
   Uranus
   Neptune
   Pluto

Five Finger Salmon

There are five species of Pacific salmon, but because most are known by multiple names it is very difficult for students to remember them all. There is, however, a simple exercise (most suitable to elementary students) that will help them learn and never forget the different species.

Using only one common name for each of the species, start with your little finger - your "pinkie". This finger represents Pink salmon (also known as Humpie). The next finger - your ring finger - can easily be associated with a silver ring, or Silver salmon (also called Coho). The middle and biggest finger on your hand is truly the king of fingers. This digit represents King Salmon (also called Spring, Tyee or Chinook). The pointer finger is next, and this is the one most likely to poke someone in the eye. Sockeye salmon (also called Red because of the blazing color change they go through at spawning time) is the most obvious association with this last finger. Finally, there is the thumb which rhymes with Chum (also called Dog) salmon.

Now reinforce this lesson with your class by showing them photos or illustrations depicting each species. Have them draw (with washable felt pens or paint) the correct salmon on each finger, or glue on cut outs (like the photo above).

Students can test their knowledge of the salmon names they have just learned by holding up, or pointing to, the correct finger as the teacher lists the different species. Once the fingers are painted, they may even enjoy doing a "fish fingers" puppet show.

Use this simple exercise to stimulate more discussion around salmon life cycles, predators and conservation issues. Which species, for instance spends the most time in the open sea? Which species spends the least time there? Could this account for the size variation between them? If so, why?

Challenge the students to name as many animals as they can that feed on salmon. There are a lot more than you would think. Finally, discuss the benefits and dangers associated with farming salmon. Is this practice ecologically sound?

There are many ways in which to expand on this simple exercise. Learning the names of species should just be a starting point for an infinitely larger and more fascinating world of discovery.

Useful Websites

Below are some of the websites that the authors have found most useful in planning lessons, conducting activities, gathering facts about Nature and conducting research.

Adopt-a-Stream
www.streamkeeper.org

American Museum of Natural History
www.amnh.org

Building Green.com
www.buildinggreen.com

Canadian Parks and Wilderness Society (CPAWS)
www.cpaws.org

Classroom Earth
www.classroomearth.org

CPAWS educational resources
www.cpawscalgary.org/education/index.html

Enchanted Learning
www.enchantedlearning.com

EnviroLink
www.envirolink.org

Green Biz.com
www.greenbiz.com

Malaysian Nature Society
www.mns.org.my

National Environmental Education and Training Foundation
www.neetf.org

North American Association For Environmental Education (NAAEE)
eelink.net

Project WET
www.projectwet.org

Rediscovery International Foundation
www.rediscovery.org

River of Words
www.riverofwords.org

Roots and Shoots
www.rootsandshoots.org

Sharing Nature Foundation
www.sharingnature.com

Thai Nature Education
www.thai-nature-ed.com

World Wildlife Fund
www.worldwildlife.org

About the Author - Thom Henley

Thom Henley has been teaching outdoor environmental education most of his adult life. He is well known for launching the largest conservation campaign in Canadian history, the 14-year effort to save the southern third of the Queen Charlotte Archipelago from clear cut logging. Today, the line on the map that he drew in 1974 is the exact boundary of the Gwaii Haanas National Park Reserve and Haida Heritage Site. The National Geographic Society recently declared Gwaii Haanas the best national park in North America.

In 1978, together with Haida elders and community members, Thom initiated the Rediscovery program. He served as Program Director for the first seven years of the camp during which time he developed most of the activities in this book. Today, with more than 40 Rediscovery camps operating throughout the world, Thom continues his work as Honorary Director of the Rediscovery International Foundation which he co-founded in 1985.

In recognition of his conservation and human rights efforts, Thom has received numerous national and international awards. He was the first person outside the USA to be the recipient of the State University of New York's prestigious Sol Feinstone Award.

Thom Henley has served on the board of the Canadian Nature Federation and is a founding director of the Islands Protection Society, Earth Life Canada and Earth Day Canada. He is an Associate Professor of the Stream Keeper Academy in Washington State where he conducts annual teacher training institutes. Recently, Thom has been appointed to the board of the Colorado-based Earth Restoration Corps.

The author has formally lectured in more than 20 countries and studied the cultures and environments of nearly 100 nations he has visited on all continents. He has been formally adopted and bestowed honorary names by the Haida, Penan, Mentawai, Newari and Tibetan indigenous peoples.

During the past decade, Thom has worked extensively with international schools throughout Asia, both in and outside the classroom. He developed the innovative 'Reefs to Rainforests' environmental education program in Thailand as well as the 'Indigenous Immersion' programs with the Moken (Sea Gypsies) of the Andaman Sea, and the Mentawai of Siberut Island, Indonesia. Thom is also involved in a long-term relief project he initiated for Burmese street-kids, many of which lost their parents to the December 26, 2004 South Asian tsunami.

Thom has published articles in numerous magazines in Asia and North America. He is the author and co-author of nine previous books: Islands At The Edge - Preserving the Queen Charlotte Islands / Rediscovery - Ancient Pathways, New Directions / Penan - Voice for the Borneo Rainforest / Reefs to Rainforests - A Guide to South Thailand's Natural Wonders / Living Legend of the Mentawai / A Seed of Hope / Waterfalls & Gibbon Calls - Exploring Khao Sok National Park / Krabi - Caught in the Spell / and River of Mist, Journey of Dreams.

About the Author - Kenny Peavy

Kenny Peavy is originally from Georgia, USA. He holds a Masters of Science in Science Education from Montana State University. He is also a certified science and math teacher with a bachelor's degree in biology from the University of Georgia. Kenny has worked extensively in ecological field studies ranging from water quality, aquatic entomology and icthyological surveys while employed at the University of Georgia's Institute of Ecology, as well as insect herbivory and plant chemical defenses through Emory University and Oak Ridge National Laboratories.

Kenny has taught thousands of students about the wonders of Nature as a naturalist in the mountains of the San Bernardino National Forest, the piedmont of Athens, Georgia, and the rainforests of Malaysia and Thailand. As a public school teacher Kenny has taught high school biology and middle school Earth science.

Kenny has also proposed and taught several courses on the natural history of Malaysia at two different international schools at both the high school and middle school level – a first for this type of course in international schools in Malaysia.

In 2001, Kenny was recognized as 'Volunteer of the Year' by the Georgia Adopt-A-Stream program for his efforts in training citizens in water quality monitoring. In 2003, Kenny was awarded a Ford Motor Company Eco-Grant to serve as founder and first chairman of the Malaysian Nature Guides to implement a volunteer amateur nature guiding program in Kuala Lumpur, Malaysia. As a result Kenny was named 'Volunteer of the Year' by the Malaysian Nature Society in 2004 for his work with the Malaysian Nature Guides.

Kenny has written and published several natural history and travel articles published online and in print in both the United States and Malaysia.

Currently, Kenny lives and teaches in Kuala Lumpur, Malaysia.

Drawing from the traditions of North American indigenous peoples, Rediscovery emerges today as a new direction for youth camps. Rediscovery, an international network of camps for native and non-native youth, focuses on personal, cultural, and environmental awareness.

"As a parent, environmentalist, and scientist, I cannot conceive of a more important program than Rediscovery — everyone in our country, old and young, should have a chance to take part. Read this book and find out what it's all about." — Dr. David Suzuki

Distributed by : Lone Pine Publishing
10145-81 AVE. Edmonton, Alberta T6E 1WG, Canada.
Tel: (780) 433-9333 Fax: (780) 433-9646

US$ 20

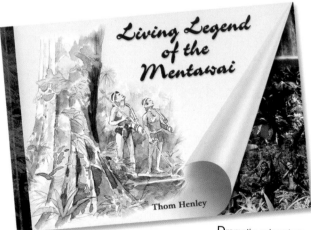

Dramatic color photos, delightful illustrations and an engaging text bring to life, for the first time, the amazing tribes people of Siberut Island, Indonesia and their living legends.

This book is much more than a portrait of a people and their profound sense of place, it is a mirror reflecting our own social values — a pulse check on humanity's heartbeat.

"Living Legend of the Mentawai" is a rare and revealing insight into one of the world's last Neolithic societies, a society that may have less to teach us about our primitive past than to inspire us in our collective future.

Distributed by : ASIA BOOKS

US$ 25

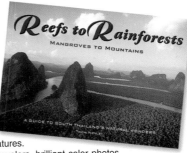

Reefs to Rainforests
MANGROVES TO MOUNTAINS

A GUIDE TO SOUTH THAILAND'S NATURAL WONDERS

Easy to read, this richly illustrated, user-friendly field guide is the perfect pocket companion for anyone wanting to know more about south Thailand's rich and varied natural environments. From the coral reefs to the inter-tidal flats, from the mangrove swamps to the darkest caves, from the evergreen tropical forests to the highest misty mountains, the award-winning author introduces the reader to more than 150 of Nature's most amazing creatures.

Detailed maps of the best places to go, tips for eco-travelers, brilliant color photos, and a passionate plea for conservation make this book both invaluable and timely.

US$ 13

Waterfalls & Gibbon Calls
EXPLORING KHAO SOK NATIONAL PARK

THOM HENLEY

Nowhere in the south of Thailand is there a larger protected area for wildlife, more stunning scenery, or more opportunities for wilderness recreation than Khao Sok National Park. And nowhere does a guide book offer you more:

-natural history
-human history
-what to bring
-detailed descriptions of flora & fauna

-complete species lists
-wildlife track guide
-health & safety tips

-how to get there
-when to go
-adventure maps & trail highlights
-suggested itineraries

The award-winning author and conservationist takes you through Khao Sok like your own personal guide.

With 88 pages of stunning color photography and beautifully hand-painted illustrations, this book will both lure you to Khao Sok and be the perfect keepsake of your journey.

Distributed by : ASIA BOOKS

US$ 11

KRABI
CAUGHT IN THE SPELL

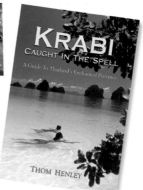

KRABI
CAUGHT IN THE SPELL
A Guide To Thailand's Enchanted Province

THOM HENLEY

A guidebook unlike any other... Thom Henley's intimate look at this enchanting province in southern Thailand is the result of more than a decade of research and personal experiences.

The author brings to life Krabi's special attractions, its fascinating peoples, and its amazingly rich natural history. Personal reflections provide insight into Thai ways and the often humorous situations foreign visitors may find themselves in.

With more than 400 stunning color images, detailed region by region maps, an extensive service directory and captivating short stories, this book is an indispensable guide for planning a trip to Krabi, a fun read while you're there, and the perfect keepsake of your journey.

Distributed by : SE-EDUCATON AND ASIA BOOKS

US$ 14

Earth Matters
Consulting Services

What happens to our planet truly does matter and, fortunately, people throughout the world are actively seeking solutions to human-generated environmental problems. Parents and educators really need to be at the forefront of this effort as their teachings will determine the values of the next generation. Whether those values lead to a more just, equitable and sustainable future for humanity and a renewed recognition of the rights of all living things, will be determined by what we teach today.

The co-authors' dedication to this cause far surpasses the publication of this book. Thom Henley has been leading outdoor education programs for students and teachers throughout the world for the past three decades. He has formally lectured on environmental education and human rights topics in 20 nations, and expanded his own knowledge of the Earth's varied ecosystems through study travel to 97 countries. Kenny Peavy, in addition to teaching Earth sciences at international schools in Asia, has also conducted a number of teacher training courses and many exciting outdoor classroom sessions for students in the USA, Malaysia and Thailand.

Both authors are available on a contract basis to serve schools, parent/teacher as-sociations, community nature clubs, scouting programs, or any group keen to learn more of the skills presented in this book. Services offered range from a 90-minute keynote address to a multiple-week immersion program. Consulting services are available for school administrators, teacher training workshops, indoor and outdoor awareness programs with students, or any other academic need.

The 'Reefs to Rainforests' program presented on pages 168 to 177 can be booked through the authors to meet the needs of a 'Week Without Walls' study program that's already built into a school's curriculum. Alternately, it can serve as a soft adventure learning vacation for students, teachers and parents during school holidays. Several times each year the program is offered as an accredited course for educators.

The Mentawai and Moken Immersion programs (pgs. 188 - 201), and the Rediscovery program (pgs. 179 - 187), can also be booked through this service. Mutang Urud, a Kelabit from Sarawak, Borneo, works with the authors as an indigenous consultant. Mutang is a globally recognized human rights and environmental champion that has lectured in many countries and currently serves as Administrator for the Rediscovery International Foundation.

CONTACTS:

Thom Henley
thomhenley@hotmail.com
Web Site:
www.thomhenley.com

Kenny Peavy
matt_salleh@hotmail.com

Mutang Urud
mutang@island.net

ACKNOWLEDGEMENTS

There are a great many people that have directly, or indirectly, contributed to this book over the course of three decades. Many of the experiential activities presented here are adapted from ones developed by co-author Thom Henley when he headed up the first Rediscovery camp on the remote shores of Haida Gwaii, Canada, in 1978. Part of that early inspiration came from some of the early pioneers in outdoor education - Garth Gilcrest, Joseph Cornell and Steve Van Mater of 'Sunship Earth' fame. Paul George and Athena George are two Canadians that encouraged the early development of these activities on Rediscovery.

Some of the exercises in this book like Storm and Water Wasters/Water Savers are the brainchilds of youth attending the annual Rediscovery International training program at Canada's United World College. Co-author Kenny Peavy developed some excellent activities for extended classroom study such as, Digital Decomposition, Follow that Pheromone, Bug Bites and others.

Both authors wish to thank the many contributors to the stewardship 'best practices' highlighted in Part III of the book: Tom Murdoch of the Stream Keeper Center in Washington State; Sven Aerts, the eco-school guru from Belgium; Amornpun Udsahakid, the economics teacher from Thailand who inspired his students to 'a bloomin good idea', and Jake Slodki who helped his students beautify a Bombay byway in India.

We are grateful to the scores of people who have allowed their images to be used in this book, and especially to our illustrators, Will Kempkes and Adul. Our heartfelt thanks goes out to Kenny's wife, Geetha, for her infinite patience, wisdom and inspiration during the writing of the book. We are also grateful to the helpful staff at Limmark Printing in Phuket, Thailand.

A hearty thanks also goes out to Callan Bentley, Adam Dodge and Rob Porter for their input, ideas and edits of various sections of the book. A special thanks to Dave Roderick for his practical approach to mathematics in a Day at the Beaver Pond and a big thanks to Kenny's colleagues and friends for their enthusiasm and support for various activities and stories they've inspired through their dedication to teaching and children.

The authors would like express our sincere gratitude to Daniel Dubie for the use of his condo on Phuket Island during the development stages of the book, and for his generous assistance in the printing.

Finally, we wish to thank all of the people whose pictures appear in these pages. Your passion for life and genuine joy in Nature shines through like a beacon welcoming us all.